Kidspiration® in the Classroom:
Reading Essentials

PHONEMIC
AWARENESS

PHONICS

VOCABULARY

COMPREHENSION

**Includes 50
Lesson Plans!**

GRADES K-5

Inspiration®
SOFTWARE, INC

CREDITS

Publisher: Mona L. Westhaver

Author: Lucy Belgum

Contributors: Mary Beth Saddoris and Andrea Sutherland

Editors: Pamela Brehm, Mary Beth Saddoris and Andrea Sutherland

Layout/Design: Kevin Jaquette

Kidspiration® in the Classroom: Reading Essentials

Inspiration Software®, Inc. strives to support improvements in education and make a positive difference in students' lives. This book is part of our family of K-12 software tools and curriculum materials that help students learn to think and master key skills and curriculum. We value teachers, their time, and their commitment, and we strive to partner in their success.

Kidspiration® in the Classroom: Reading Essentials supports teachers as they help students develop the critical thinking strategies and reading skills that are fundamental to literacy.

Covering two grade spans, K–2 and 3–5, the *Kidspiration in the Classroom: Reading Essentials* lesson plan book offers 50 standards-based lesson plans designed specifically to support K–5 reading instruction using Kidspiration 3.

Lessons for grades K–2 focus on early literacy and the essential components of effective reading instruction, including phonemic awareness, phonics, vocabulary and comprehension. For grades 3–5, the lessons focus on teaching comprehension, vocabulary and content literacy.

Each easy-to-use lesson includes standards alignment, lesson description and step-by-step instructions. Phonemic awareness, phonics and vocabulary lessons also include teaching suggestions to support English language learners.

Reading Essentials Resources

Allington, Richard. 2001. *What Really Matters for Struggling Readers: Designing Research-Based Programs*. New York: Addison Wesley.

Harvey, Stephanie and Anne Goudvis. 2000. *Strategies That Work: Teaching Comprehension to Enhance Understanding*. Portland, ME: Stenhouse.

2007. *Strategies That Work: Teaching Comprehension to Enhance Understanding*. 2nd ed. Portland, ME: Stenhouse.

Kendall, J.S. and Marzano, R.J. 2008. *Content knowledge: A compendium of standards and benchmarks for K-12 education*. Denver, CO: Mid-continent Research for Education and Learning. Online database: http://www.mcrel.org/standards-benchmarks/

Miller, Debbie. 2002. *Teaching Comprehension in the Primary Grades*. Portland, ME: Stenhouse.

Pinnell, Gay Sue and Irene C. Fountas. 2003. *Phonics Lessons: Letters, Words, and How They Work*. Portsmouth, NH: Heineman.

TABLE OF CONTENTS

K-2 Phonemic Awareness

K-2 Phonics

K-2 Vocabulary

K-2 Comprehension

TABLE OF CONTENTS

3-5 Vocabulary

3-5 Comprehension

Blending Phonemes

Standards

✳ McREL Standards – Language Arts

(http://www.mcrel.org/standards-benchmarks/)

- Discriminates among the sounds of spoken language
- Listens for a variety of purposes

✳ Grade Levels: K-2 (Ages 5-8)

Description

Phonemic awareness is the ability to hear, identify and manipulate individual sounds in spoken words. Hearing the word *cat* for example, and identifying the word as having three sounds or phonemes, *k/a/t*, is a phonemic awareness skill. Phonemic awareness skills include: word segmentation, rhyming, phoneme matching, awareness of syllables, and phoneme blending and manipulation. In addition to helping students improve comprehension and organize ideas for writing, Kidspiration® can be used as a tool to help students learn, practice and apply specific phonemic awareness skills, supporting the teacher's reading curriculum. This Kidspiration activity allows young learners the opportunity to hear and blend individual phonemes.

Instructions

1. Prior to beginning the lesson below, read aloud a book that emphasizes sounds. Read the words slowly so students hear all the sounds. Suggestions are: *Boats* by Byron Barton and *To Market, To Market* by Anne Miranda. Share with students that today they will learn more about the sounds in words so they can use them in their reading and writing like the author of the book just read.

2. Go to **Kidspiration 3 Teacher menu>Teacher Resources Online>Lesson Plans** and open the *Blending Phonemes 3.kia* activity. Explain to students that they will use this activity to blend word sounds together.

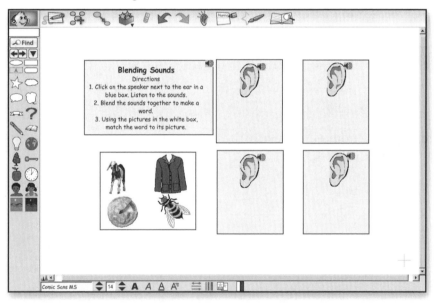

   Explain that you will show them how to use the activity before they use it on their own. After showing students the activity, close the activity.

3. Create a new Kidspiration activity in **Picture View**. Select a word to model blending individual phonemes, represented by a symbol in the **Symbol palette**, e.g., *dog, cat, boat*. Place the symbol on the activity. Say the name of the symbol, segmenting each phoneme or sound in the word. Then model blending the sounds together, naming the symbol. Continue using several examples until the skill has been demonstrated sufficiently, gradually moving from demonstration for students to guided practice by the students.

4. Return to the *Blending Phonemes 3.kia* activity. Explain to students that they will now practice what they have learned about blending sounds to complete the activity independently. Point out to students that in the direction box is a speaker icon. Demonstrate clicking on it to listen to the directions for the activity. Students will also click on speaker icons to hear the individual sounds of the words. Demonstrate this, pointing out that students may replay the word sounds as often as they wish.

5. Show students how to complete the activity by clicking on a speaker icon, listening to the sounds, blending the sounds and dragging a picture of the word heard to the box associated with the word sounds. When finished, have students complete the activity independently.

Additional phonemic awareness activities, including blending phonemes, can be located here: **Kidspiration 3 Teacher menu>Teacher Resources Online>Lesson Plans.**

Assessment

-   Confirm that students have completed the activity, matching the pictures with the correct segmented words.

Adaptations

- The activity may be printed after its completion and used as an informal assessment.

- The activity may be used in a literacy center. Print a copy of the *Blending Phonemes 3.kid* activity shown below. Place the printed version in the center; instruct students on how to self-check their work.

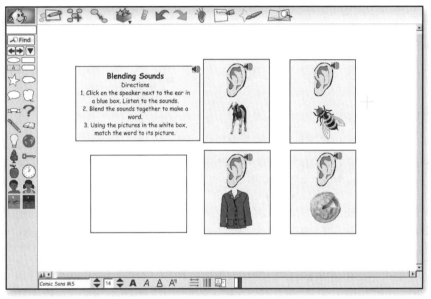

English Language Learners

Provide English language learners with opportunities to blend words that are known and meaningful to them. Selecting familiar symbols during the modeling portion of the lesson will provide additional support. Students will need to understand the abstract concept of individual word sounds and thus may need several demonstrations on blending phonemes. Given that precise pronunciations can be difficult, accept approximations and praise students for their efforts.

Blending Onsets and Rimes

Standards

✴ McREL Standards – Language Arts

(http://www.mcrel.org/standards-benchmarks/)

- Discriminates among the sounds of spoken language
- Listens for a variety of purposes

✴ Grade Levels: K-2 (Ages 5-8)

Description

Phonemic awareness is the ability to hear, identify and manipulate individual sounds in spoken words. Hearing the word *cat* for example, and identifying the word as having three sounds or phonemes, *k/a/t*, is a phonemic awareness skill. Phonemic awareness skills include: word segmentation, rhyming, phoneme matching, awareness of syllables, and phoneme blending and manipulation. In addition to helping students improve comprehension and organize ideas for writing, Kidspiration® can be used as a tool to help students learn, practice and apply specific phonemic awareness skills, supporting the teacher's reading curriculum.

Syllables are easy word parts for children to recognize and are easily taught by having the students clap the number of word parts or syllables heard while saying the word. Syllables can be divided into the onset (the letters before the vowel) and the rime (the vowel and whatever letters come after it). This Kidspiration activity allows young learners the opportunity to hear and blend word parts.

Instructions

1. Prior to beginning the lesson, read aloud a book that emphasizes rhyming words. Suggestions are: *I Heard a Little Baa* by Elizabeth MacLeod and *These Little Hands* by Hope Lynne Price. Share with students that today they will learn more about the sounds of letters so they can use them in their reading and writing like the author of the book just read.

   Note: Prior to this lesson, it is important that children understand the concept of first and last as it relates to the sequence of sounds. The terms "onset" and "rime" are not necessary terms for children to know.

2. Go to **Kidspiration 3 Teacher menu>Teacher Resources Online>Lesson Plans** and open the *Onsets and Rimes 2.kia* activity, shown below.

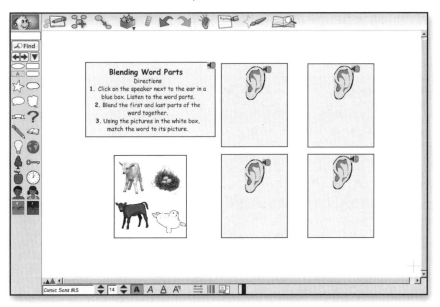

   Explain to students that they will use this activity to blend word parts together at the end of the lesson. Explain that you will show them how to use the activity before they use it on their own. After showing students the activity, close the activity.

3. Create a new Kidspiration activity in **Picture View**. Select a word to model blending the onset and rime, represented by a symbol in the **Symbol palette**, e.g., *snake, train, top*. Place the symbol on the activity. Separating the onset and rime, say the name of the symbol. Then model blending the word parts together, naming the symbol. Next say the onset and rime,

having the students blend and say the complete word. While modeling the skill, gradually move from demonstration for students to guided practice by the students.

4. Return to the *Onsets and Rimes 2.kia* activity. Explain to students that they will now practice what they have learned about blending word parts to complete the activity independently. Point out to students that in the directions box is a speaker icon. Demonstrate clicking on it to listen to the directions for the activity. Students will also click on speaker icons to hear the individual sounds of the words. Demonstrate this, pointing out that students may replay the word sounds as often as they wish.

5. Show students how to complete the activity by clicking on a speaker icon, listening to the sounds, blending the sounds and dragging a picture of the word heard to the box associated with the word sounds.

6. Demonstrate how to drag the picture back to the white box should the student wish to do so.

7. Once directions have been given, students may complete the activity independently.

Additional phonemic awareness activities, including blending onsets and rimes, can be located here: **Kidspiration 3 Teacher menu>Teacher Resources Online>Lesson Plans.**

Assessment
-   Confirm that students have completed the activity, matching the pictures with the correct word parts.

Adaptations

- The activity may be printed after its completion and used as an informal assessment.

- The activity may be used in a literacy center. Print a copy of the *Onsets Rimes Exemplar 2.kid* activity shown below. Place the printed version in the center; instruct students on how to self-check their work.

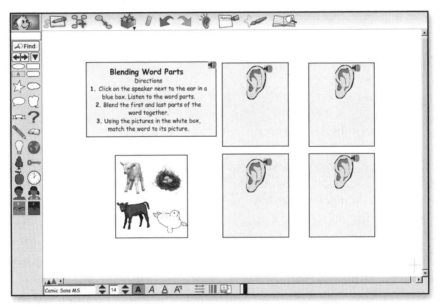

English Language Learners

Provide English language learners with opportunities to rhyme words that are known and meaningful to them. Selecting familiar symbols during the modeling portion of the lesson will provide additional support.

Hearing Beginning Phonemes

Standards

✦ McREL Standards – Language Arts

(http://www.mcrel.org/standards-benchmarks/)

- Discriminates among the sounds of spoken language
- Listens for a variety of purposes

✦ Grade Levels: K-2 (Ages 5-8)

Description

Phonemic awareness is the ability to hear, identify and manipulate individual sounds in spoken words. Hearing the word *cat* for example, and identifying the word as having three sounds or phonemes, *k/a/t*, is a phonemic awareness skill. Phonemic awareness skills include: word segmentation, rhyming, phoneme matching, awareness of syllables, and phoneme blending and manipulation. In addition to helping students improve comprehension and organize ideas for writing, Kidspiration® can be used as a tool to help students learn, practice and apply specific phonemic awareness skills, supporting the teacher's reading curriculum.

Students need to be able to say a word and match other words that have the same beginning (or ending) sound. This skill is essential if students are going to associate the sounds in words with letters. In this Kidspiration activity, young learners will identify pictures that have the same beginning sounds.

Instructions

1. Prior to beginning the lesson below, read aloud a book with alliteration. Suggestions are: *Tomorrow's Alphabet* by George Shannon and *Alphabet Under Construction* by Denise Fleming. Share with students that today they will learn more about beginning sounds in words so they can use them in their reading and writing like the author of the book just read.

2. Go to **Kidspiration 3 Teacher menu>Teacher Resources Online>Lesson Plans** and open the *Begin Phonemes b.kia* activity, shown below. Explain to students that they will use this activity to identify pictures that have the same beginning sounds.

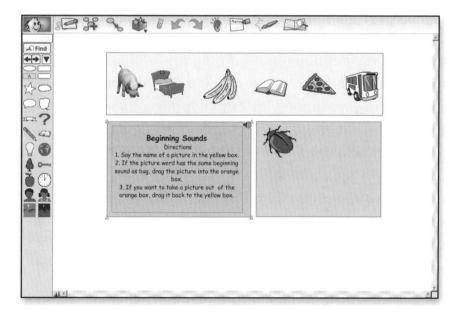

Explain that you will show them how to use the activity before they use it on their own. After showing students the activity, close the activity.

3. Create a new Kidspiration activity in **Picture View**. In order as listed, select the following symbols from the *Animals & Plants* symbol libraries, placing them randomly on the activity: *dog, bird, lion, donkey, llama, cat, cougar* and *bear*. Click on the *bear* symbol. Say the word "bear" several times, emphasizing the beginning sound. Explain to students that you want to find another picture that has the same first sound as "bear." Click on the remainder of the pictures, one at a time, saying the picture name and emphasizing the beginning sound

until saying the word "bird." Then model language similar to the following: "Bear, bah, bear. Bird, bah, bird. Yes, they both have the first sound of 'bah.'" Drag the two pictures side-by-side. Match the remainder of the pictures in the same manner. Gradually move from demonstration for students to guided practice by the students.

4. Return to the *Begin Phonemes b.kia* activity. Explain to students that they will now practice what they have learned about beginning sounds in words to complete the activity independently. Demonstrate for students how to click on the speaker icon to listen to the directions for the activity, pointing out that they may listen to the directions as often as needed.

5. Show students how to complete the activity by dragging a picture from the yellow box that has the same first sound as the picture in the orange box.

6. Demonstrate how to drag a picture back to the yellow box should the student not wish to have the picture in the orange box.

7. Once directions have been given, students may complete the activity independently.

Additional phonemic awareness activities, including identifying other beginning phoneme activities, can be located here: **Kidspiration 3 Teacher menu>Teacher Resources Online>Lesson Plans.**

Assessment
- Confirm that students have completed the activity, matching pictures with the same beginning sound.

Adaptations
- The activity may be printed after its completion and used as an informal assessment.

- The activity may be used in a literacy center. Print a copy of the *Begin Phonemes Exemplar.kid* activity shown below. Place the printed version in the center; instruct students on how to self-check their work.

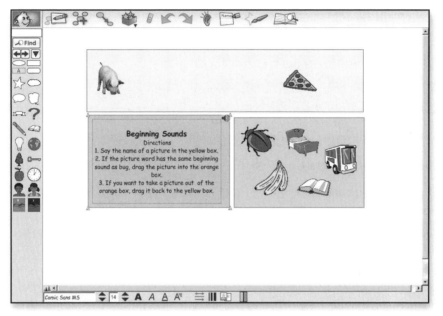

- Select several symbols with the same beginning sound in an activity. Print the activity. Have students cut the symbols out and match the symbols that have the same first sound. Students may place the cut out symbols in an envelope and take them home for additional practice.

English Language Learners

Provide English language learners with opportunities to learn and practice the skill using words and symbols that are familiar to them. Practice saying the words several times, emphasizing the beginning sound, being careful however not to distort it. Students may need help in understanding the concept of "first sound" and need several demonstrations. Have students attend to what their mouths are doing when saying the first sound of the picture. Given that precise pronunciations can be difficult, accept approximations and praise students for their efforts.

Recognizing Rhymes

Standards

✦ McREL Standards – Language Arts

(http://www.mcrel.org/standards-benchmarks/)

- Discriminates among the sounds of spoken language
- Listens for a variety of purposes
- Knows rhyming sounds and simple rhymes

✦ Grade Levels: K-2 (Ages 5-8)

Description

Phonemic awareness is the ability to hear, identify and manipulate individual sounds in spoken words. Hearing the word *cat* for example, and identifying the word as having three sounds or phonemes, *k/a/t*, is a phonemic awareness skill. Phonemic awareness skills include: word segmentation, rhyming, phoneme matching, awareness of syllables, and phoneme blending and manipulation. In addition to helping students improve comprehension and organize ideas for writing, Kidspiration® can be used as a tool to help students learn, practice and apply specific phonemic awareness skills, supporting the teacher's reading curriculum.

When students are able to identify words that rhyme, it helps them become aware of the sequence of sounds in words, hearing not only individual sounds, but clusters of sounds as well. This Kidspiration activity allows young learners the opportunity to identify names of pictures that rhyme.

Instructions

1. Prior to beginning the lesson below, read aloud in a fun manner a book that rhymes. Suggestions are: *One Duck Stuck* by Phyllis Root and *Pigs in the Mud* by Lynn Plourde. Share with students that today they will learn more about rhyming words so they can use what they know about ending sounds in their reading and writing like the author of the book just read.

2. Go to **Kidspiration 3 Teacher menu>Teacher Resources Online>Lesson Plans** and open the *Recognizing Rhymes 3.kia* activity, shown below. Explain to students that they will use this activity to match rhyming words, i.e., words with the same ending sounds. Explain that you will show them how to use the activity before they complete it on their own. After showing students the activity, close the activity.

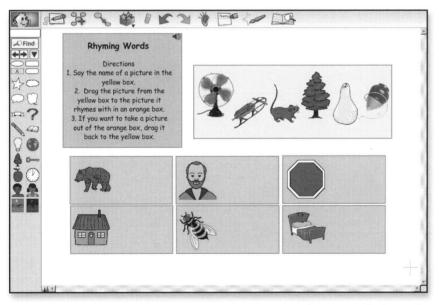

3. Create a new Kidspiration activity in **Picture View**. Perform a symbol search to find the following symbols in the Kidspiration **Symbol palette**: *duck, fox, zoo, box, glue, truck, bee* and *tree*. Place them randomly on the workspace. Let students know they will be learning about words that rhyme. Drag the *tree* and *bee* symbols side-by-side. Point out as you say the names of the pictures that the two words rhyme and have the same ending sound. Have the students say the names of the symbols as well. Model using the remainder of the symbols in a similar manner. While modeling the skill, gradually move from demonstration for students to guided practice by the students.

4. Return to the *Recognizing Rhymes 3.kia* activity. Together, name the symbols in the activity. Explain to students that they will now practice what they have learned about rhyming words and complete the activity independently. Demonstrate for students how to click on the speaker icon to listen to the directions for the activity, pointing out that students may replay the directions as often as they wish. Demonstrate also how to drag a symbol to a box.

5. Once directions have been given, students may complete the activity independently.

Additional phonemic awareness activities, including other rhyming activities, can be located here: **Kidspiration 3 Teacher menu>Teacher Resources Online>Lesson Plans.**

Assessment
- Confirm that students have completed the activity, matching the symbols that rhyme.

Adaptations

- The activity may be printed after its completion and used as an informal assessment.

- The activity may be used in a literacy center. Print a copy of the *Rhymes Exemplar 3.kid* activity shown below. Place the printed version in the center; instruct students on how to self-check their work.

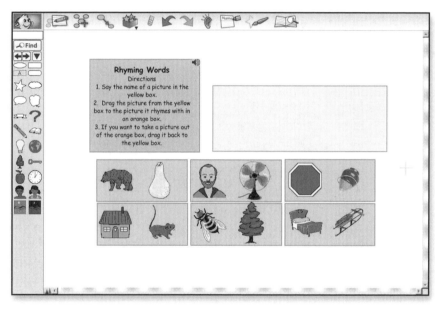

- Select several symbols which rhyme and place them in an activity. Print the activity. Have students cut the symbols out and match the symbols that rhyme. Students may place the cut out symbols in an envelope and take them home to continue to practice the skill.

English Language Learners

Provide English language learners with opportunities to rhyme words that are known and meaningful to them. Selecting familiar symbols during the modeling portion of the lesson will provide additional support.

Identifying Number of Syllables

Standards

⭐ **McREL Standards – Language Arts**

(http://www.mcrel.org/standards-benchmarks/)

- Discriminates among the sounds of spoken language
- Listens for a variety of purposes
- Knows that words are made up of syllables

⭐ **Grade Levels: K-2 (Ages 5-8)**

Description

Phonemic awareness is the ability to hear, identify and manipulate individual sounds in spoken words. Hearing the word *cat* for example, and identifying the word as having three sounds or phonemes, *k/a/t*, is a phonemic awareness skill. Phonemic awareness skills include: word segmentation, rhyming, phoneme matching, awareness of syllables, and phoneme blending and manipulation. In addition to helping students improve comprehension and organize ideas for writing, Kidspiration® can be used as a tool to help students learn, practice and apply specific phonemic awareness skills, supporting the teacher's reading curriculum.

The structure of syllables in words helps students hear sounds and identify the number of syllables within a word. Each syllable contains an onset (the letters before the vowel) and a rime (the vowel and letters that follow). A syllable can be an entire word like *to* or a word may contain several syllables like *necessary*. This Kidspiration activity allows young learners the opportunity to identify the number of syllables in a word.

Note: Students do not need to be familiar with the words "onset" and "rime" for this lesson.

Instructions

1. Prior to beginning the lesson below, read aloud a book that has several character names and have the students clap the syllables in the names. Suggestions are: *Safe, Warm and Snug* by Stephen Swinburne and *Ms. Bindergarten Celebrates the 100th Day of Kindergarten* by Joseph Slate. Share with students that today they will learn more about word parts so they can use them in their reading and writing like the author of the book just read.

2. Go to **Kidspiration 3 Teacher menu>Teacher Resources Online>Lesson Plans** and open the *Syllables 1&2.kia* activity, shown below. Explain to students that they will use this activity to identify the number of syllables in words at the end of the lesson. Explain that you will show them how to use the activity before they use it on their own. After showing students the activity, close the activity.

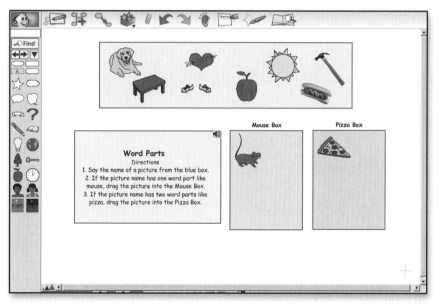

3. Create a new Kidspiration activity in **Picture View**. Select the following symbols from the *Fruits & Veggies* library under *Food & Health*, placing them randomly on the activity: *apple, mushroom, pear, grapes, bananas, pumpkin, corn, peas, potato* and *broccoli*. Let students know they will be learning about word parts. Click on the *apple* symbol. Say the word and demonstrate clapping the word into syllables. Have the students say "apple," clapping the word into syllables. Model using the remainder of the symbols in a similar manner. While modeling the skill, gradually move from demonstration for students to guided practice by the students.

4. Return to the *Syllables 1&2.kia* activity. Together, name the symbols in the activity. Explain to students that they will now practice what they have learned about clapping words into syllables and complete the activity independently. Demonstrate for students how to click on the speaker icon to listen to the directions for the activity, pointing out that students may replay the directions as often as they wish. Demonstrate also how to drag a symbol to a box.

5. Once directions have been given, students may complete the activity independently.

Additional phonemic awareness activities, including other syllable activities, can be located here: **Kidspiration 3 Teacher menu>Teacher Resources Online>Lesson Plans.**

Assessment

- Confirm that students have completed the activity, placing the symbols into the correct boxes.

Adaptations

- The activity may be printed after its completion and used as an informal assessment.

- The activity may be used in a literacy center. Print a copy of the *Syllables Exemplar.kid* activity shown below. Place the printed version in the center; instruct students on how to self-check their work.

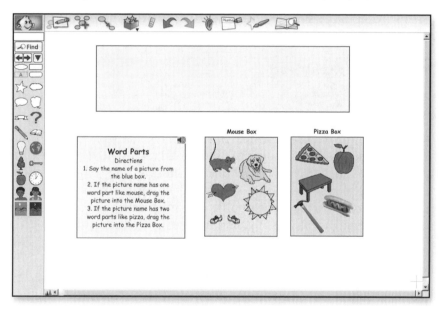

- Select several symbols containing 1-3 syllables and place them in an activity. Print the activity. Have students cut the symbols out and group the pictures by the number of syllables in each word. Students may place the cut out symbols in an envelope and take them home to continue to practice the skill.

English Language Learners

English language learners will need to understand the concept of word parts. Provide several opportunities for them to practice clapping the syllables, using words that are meaningful to them. As pronunciation of words may be difficult, accept approximations and praise the students for their attempts.

Beginning Consonant Clusters

Standards

✦ McREL Standards – Language Arts

(http://www.mcrel.org/standards-benchmarks/)

- Uses the general skills and strategies of the reading process
- Uses basic elements of phonetic analysis

✦ Grade Levels: K-2 (Ages 5-8)

Description

Phonics is the relationship between phonemes (sounds) and graphemes (letters/spellings that represent sounds). It is how the sounds of speech are represented by letters; students use the rules of phonics to read and write. Phonics includes an array of graphophonemic skills. In addition to helping students improve comprehension and organize ideas for writing, Kidspiration® can be used as a tool to help students learn, practice and apply specific phonics skills, supporting the teacher's reading curriculum.

In this Kidspiration activity, young learners will identify which consonant clusters begin names of pictures.

Note: This lesson is suitable for students who know most of the consonants and their sounds.

Instructions

1. Prior to beginning the lesson below, read aloud a book that emphasizes the repetition of letter clusters. Suggestions are: *Get to Work, Trucks* by Don Carter or *I Stink* by Kate McCullan. Share with students that today they will learn more about groups of beginning letters so they can use them in their reading and writing like the author of the book just read.

2. Go to **Kidspiration 3 Teacher menu>Teacher Resources Online>Lesson Plans** and open the *Begin Consonant Clusters.kia* activity, shown below. Explain to students that they will use this activity to identify a consonant cluster, i.e., a group of two consonants, that begin the name of a picture.

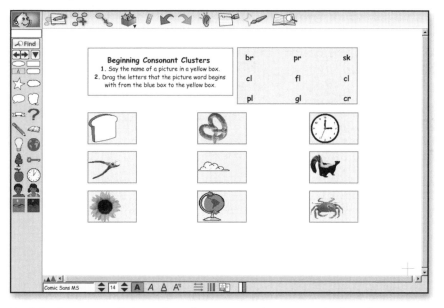

Explain that you will show them how to use the activity before they use it on their own. After showing students the activity, close the activity.

3. Create a new Kidspiration activity in **Picture View**. Share with students that they have been learning a lot about consonants and the sounds associated with them. Today they will learn about some consonants that go together in words and they are called *consonant clusters*. Select the *tree* symbol from the *Basic* library in the **Symbol palette**, placing it on the activity. Ask the students to name the symbol. Write *tree* under the symbol. Explain that *tree* starts with *t* and the next letter is *r*. *T* and *r* go together in many words and the *tr* is called a *consonant cluster*. Other words that *tr* go together in are: *trike, trash, train, trip*. (Write these

words on the activity as they are said.) Help the students understand that they hear both the *t* and the *r* in the word *tree*. Depending on the skill level of the students, decide whether to model in the same manner other consonant clusters, e.g., *fl, cl, br, cr*. While modeling the skill, gradually move from demonstration for students to guided practice by the students.

4. Return to the *Begin Consonant Clusters.kia* activity. Explain to students that they will now practice what they have learned about consonant clusters and complete the activity independently. Demonstrate for students how to use the **Listen** tool to listen to the directions if necessary. Show students how to drag a consonant cluster to a picture.

5. Once directions have been given, students may complete the activity independently.

Additional phonics activities can be located here: **Kidspiration 3 Teacher menu>Teacher Resources Online>Lesson Plans.**

Assessment

- Confirm that students have completed the activity, matching the consonant clusters with the correct pictures.

- Observe if students represent both sounds in consonant clusters when writing.

- Observe if students use both sounds in consonant clusters to self-monitor when reading.

Adaptations

- The activity may be printed after its completion and used as an informal assessment.

- The activity may be used in a literacy center. Print a copy of the *Consonant Clusters Exemplar.kid* activity shown below. Place the printed version in the center; instruct students on how to self-check their work.

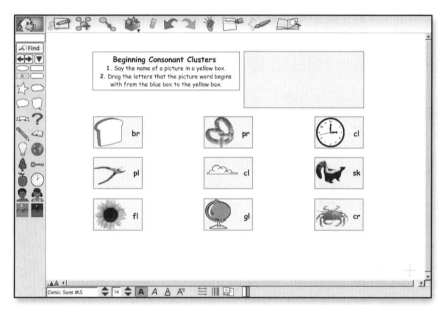

English Language Learners

Prior to using this lesson with English language learners, make sure students can identify individual consonant letters and the sounds they represent. Use words and pictures they are familiar with and can pronounce. Often the *tr* cluster will sound like *ch* to English language learners, thus it is important to say the words slowly. Have the students repeat the words while looking at the letters.

Spelling CVC Pattern Words

Standards

✶ McREL Standards – Language Arts

(http://www.mcrel.org/standards-benchmarks/)

- Uses the general skills and strategies of the reading process
- Uses basic elements of phonetic analysis

✶ Grade Levels: K-2 (Ages 5-8)

Description

Phonics is the relationship between phonemes (sounds) and graphemes (letters/spellings that represent sounds). It is how the sounds of speech are represented by letters; students use the rules of phonics to read and write. Phonics includes an array of graphophonemic skills. In addition to helping students improve comprehension and organize ideas for writing, Kidspiration® can be used as a tool to help students learn, practice and apply specific phonics skills, supporting the teacher's reading curriculum.

As students learn more about vowel sounds and their positions within words, they increase their ability to decode and spell more effectively. In this Kidspiration activity, young learners will learn to spell consonant-vowel-consonant (CVC) patterned words.

Note: This lesson is suitable for students who know the term *short vowel* and the sounds associated with the short vowels *a, e, i, o* and *u*. Students also need to be able to hear and identify beginning, middle and ending sounds.

Instructions

1. Prior to beginning the lesson, read aloud a book that contains words having the CVC spelling pattern and point out several of the words. Suggestions are: *Moonlight Kite* by Helen Buckley or *The Table Where Rich People Live* by Byrd Baylor. Share with students that today they will learn more about groups of beginning letters and short vowel spelling patterns so they can use them in their reading and writing like the author of the book just read.

2. Go to **Kidspiration 3 Teacher menu>Teacher Resources Online>Lesson Plans** and open the *CVC Pattern Words.kia* activity, shown below. Explain to students that they will use this activity to spell words that name a picture.

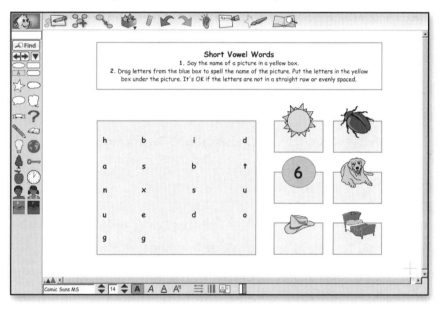

Explain that you will show them how to use the activity before they use it on their own. After showing students the activity, close the activity.

3. Create a new Kidspiration activity in **Picture View**. Share with the students that they have been learning a lot about consonant and vowel sounds. Explain that vowels can have two sounds; a long vowel sound like the letter's name, like the *i* in *bike*, or a short vowel sound that is different than the sound of its name, like the *i* in *big*. Today they will learn about short vowel sound spelling patterns. It is also called the *consonant-vowel-consonant rule*. Select the *dog, cat* and *rat* symbols from the *Animal & Plants* libraries in the **Symbol palette**, placing them on the activity. Click on the *dog* symbol and ask the students to name the

symbol. Together, listen for and write the beginning, middle and ending letters of the word. Using the remainder of the symbols, model using the same procedure. Point out to students that all three words follow the same spelling pattern, consonant-vowel-consonant, and in all three cases the vowel has the short sound. Explain that this is a spelling pattern and it will help them read and spell many words. Demonstrate the spelling pattern again using other symbols familiar to students which follow the CVC spelling pattern. While modeling the skill, gradually move from demonstration for students to guided practice by the students.

4. Return to the *CVC Pattern Words.kia* activity. Explain to students that they will now practice what they have learned about the CVC spelling pattern to complete the activity independently. Demonstrate for students how to use the **Listen** tool to listen to the directions if necessary. Show students how to drag letters from the blue box to the yellow boxes. Explain to students that the letters need to be in the correct order, but having the letters neatly in a row is not important.

5. Remind students that this lesson will help them read and write CVC pattern words more easily. Once directions have been given, students may complete the activity independently.

Additional phonics activities can be located here: **Kidspiration 3 Teacher menu>Teacher Resources Online>Lesson Plans.**

Assessment

- Confirm that students have completed the activity, placing the letters correctly.
- Observe if students are able to use the CVC pattern when writing.
- Observe if students use the CVC pattern to self-monitor when reading.

Adaptations

- The activity may be printed after its completion and used as an informal assessment.

- The activity may be used in a literacy center. Print a copy of the *CVC Pattern Words Exemplar.kid* activity shown below. Place the printed version in the center; instruct students on how to self-check their work.

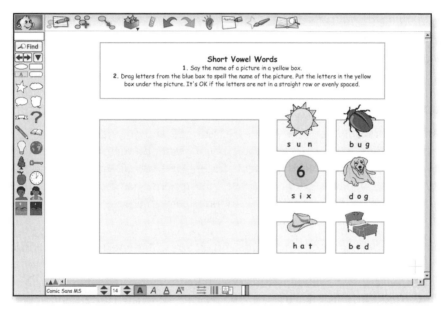

English Language Learners

This lesson will help English language learners listen carefully to consonant and vowel sounds, and help them to differentiate between the vowel sounds. Use the term *vowel* and teach them to identify the five primary vowels. Show students how to pronounce the words, exaggerating the vowel sounds slightly without distorting the sounds, and work with them until they can say the words independently. The words used should be in the students' speaking vocabulary.

Identifying Initial Sounds and Letters

Standards

✦ McREL Standards – Language Arts

(http://www.mcrel.org/standards-benchmarks/)

- Uses the general skills and strategies of the reading process
- Uses basic elements of phonetic analysis

✦ Grade Levels: K-2 (Ages 5-8)

Description

Phonics is the relationship between phonemes (sounds) and graphemes (letters/spellings that represent sounds). Phonics includes an array of graphophonemic skills. It is how the sounds of speech are represented by letters; students use the rules of phonics to read and write. In addition to helping students improve comprehension and organize ideas for writing, Kidspiration® can be used as a tool to help students learn, practice and apply specific phonics skills, supporting the teacher's reading curriculum.

Letter sounds can be associated with words and pictures. Students say a word and identify the first sound, while they identify the letter and connect the letter to its sound. When students are able to use this skill, they begin to use the letter/beginning sound relationship when reading and writing. In this Kidspiration activity, young learners will match letters and initial sounds of words with pictures.

Instructions

1. Select and read an alphabet book to the class. After reading, discuss how the book had a picture for each letter of the alphabet. Explain how the author matched the beginning letters and sounds with the pictures or illustrations in the book.

2. Go to **Kidspiration 3 Teacher menu>Teacher Resources Online>Lesson Plans** and open the *Alphabet Sounds.kia* activity. Explain to students that they will use this activity to match letters and sounds with pictures and make their own alphabet cards much like the author of the book just read. Explain that you will show them how to use the activity before they use it on their own.

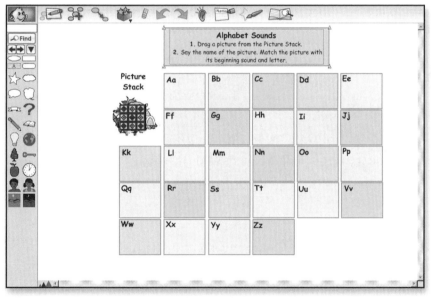

3. Share with students that they have been learning about letters and sounds and today they will learn more. Select a letter whose shape, name and related sound most students know. With the *Alphabet Sounds.kia* activity open, select a symbol from a library in the **Symbol palette** (not from the *Picture Stack*) that begins with the letter, and say, for example, "This is a door. Say the word *door* with me. I'm going to put the picture of the door under the letter *d* because you can hear the "dah" sound at the beginning of the word. This is a dog. Say the word *dog* with me. Where would I place the picture of the dog?" Model using other familiar letters and sounds, gradually moving from demonstration for students to guided practice by the students.

4. Explain to students that they will now practice what they have learned about matching letters and sounds in words to complete the activity independently. Demonstrate for students how to use the **Listen** tool to listen to the directions if necessary. Show students how to take a picture from the *Picture Stack* portion of the activity and place it in a letter card.

5. Remind students that knowing the letters and sounds at the beginning of words will help them to read and write. Once directions have been given, students may complete the activity independently.

Additional phonics activities can be located here: **Kidspiration 3 Teacher menu>Teacher Resources Online>Lesson Plans**.

Assessment

- Confirm that students have completed the activity, matching the pictures with the correct beginning letters.

- Observe if students use the correct beginning letters when writing.

- Observe if students use beginning sounds when reading.

Adaptations

- The activity may be printed after its completion and used as an informal assessment.

- The students may print the alphabet cards, keeping a copy at their desks, to assist them in reading and writing.

- The activity may be used in a literacy center. Print a copy of the *Sounds Exemplar.kid* activity shown below. Place the printed version in the center; instruct students on how to self-check their work.

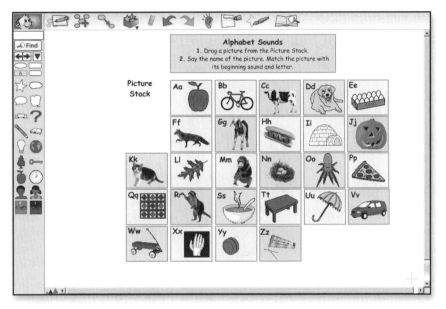

- Rather than using teacher-selected symbols when demonstrating the skill as explained in #3 under Instructions, the teacher may elect to use the symbols from the *Picture Stack*.

- The activity may be used in Guided Reading groups with students who need additional experience with matching letters and beginning sounds of words.

English Language Learners

This lesson will help develop English language learners' speaking and listening vocabularies as well as help them to match letters and sounds. Students will need to know the names of the pictures prior to completing the activity. In a small group prior to teaching the lesson, teach and/or review the names of the pictures used in the activity. Say the name of the picture and have students repeat it.

Recognizing Short Vowel Sounds

Standards

✴ McREL Standards – Language Arts

(http://www.mcrel.org/standards-benchmarks/)

- Uses the general skills and strategies of the reading process
- Uses basic elements of phonetic analysis

✴ Grade Levels: K-2 (Ages 5-8)

Description

Phonics is the relationship between phonemes (sounds) and graphemes (letters/spellings that represent sounds). Phonics includes an array of graphophonemic skills. It is how the sounds of speech are represented by letters; students use the rules of phonics to read and write.
In addition to helping students improve comprehension and organizing ideas for writing, Kidspiration® can be used as a tool to help students learn, practice and apply specific phonics skills, supporting the teachers' reading curriculum.

Students need many exposures to vowels to become familiar with common vowel patterns. In this Kidspiration activity, young learners will recognize and identify short vowel sounds. This lesson is effective with students who know and have worked with the five vowels and have looked at short vowel sounds, one at a time.

Instructions

1. Go to **Kidspiration 3 Teacher menu>Teacher Resources Online>Lesson Plans** and open the *Short Vowel Sounds.kia* template, shown below. Explain to students that they will use this activity to identify which short vowel sound is heard in a word.

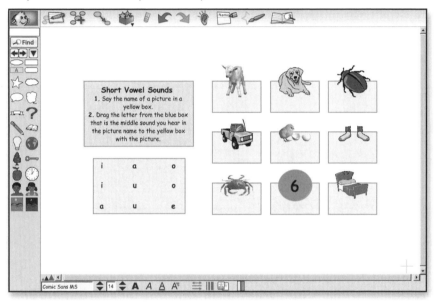

Explain that you will show them how to use the activity before they use it on their own. After showing students the activity, close the activity.

2. Share with the students that they have been learning about vowel sounds. They know vowels can have two sounds. It can have a sound like its name, like *i* as in *bike*. That is called a *long vowel sound*. A vowel can also have a different sound from its name, like the *i* in *big*. That is called a *short vowel sound*. Today they will learn more about short vowel sounds.

3. Create a new Kidspiration activity in **Picture View**. Perform a **Symbol Search** to find the following symbols in the Kidspiration **Symbol palette**: the numbers *6* and *10, bus, man, mug, rat, net, pig, fox* and *dog*. Place them on the left side of the activity. Type the five vowels, *a, e, i, o* and *u,* in 18 point font and place them at the top of the activity. An example of the activity is shown below.

Use language similar to the following to teach the lesson: "Today we are going to listen for short vowel sounds in words. Listen to the names of these pictures: *six, ten, bus, man, mug, rat, net, pig, fox* and *dog*. (Point to the pictures as the words are said.) All of these picture names have a short vowel sound. A short vowel sound is different than the vowels' name. (Click on the *rat* symbol.) Listen to the word *rat*. Say the word *rat* with me. The word *rat* has the short *a* vowel sound. (Drag the *rat* symbol under the letter *a*.) What other picture has the same short vowel sound as *rat*? (After students have identified the picture of the *man* as having a short *a* vowel sound, drag the *man* symbol under the picture of the *rat*.) Use the remainder of the symbols, using similar language, gradually moving from demonstration for students to guided practice by the students.

4. Explain to students that they will now practice what they have learned about matching letters to the short vowel sounds heard in words to complete the activity independently. Open the *Short Vowel Sounds.kia* template again. Demonstrate for students how to use the **Listen** tool to listen to the directions if necessary and how to drag a letter from the blue box to a yellow box. Remind students that knowing the short vowel sounds and their letters will help them become better readers and writers. Once directions have been given, students may complete the activity independently.

Additional phonics activities can be located here: **Kidspiration 3 Teacher menu>Teacher Resources Online>Lesson Plans.**

Assessment

- Confirm that students have completed the activity, placing the correct letter under the picture.

- Observe if students use the correct letter for given short vowel sounds in writing.

- Observe if students use the correct short vowel sound for a given letter when reading.

Adaptations

- The activity may be printed after its completion and used as an informal assessment.

- Students may switch to **Writing View** after completing the activity and write the picture word in its entirety. Additionally, students may use the word in a sentence.

- The activity may be used in a literacy center. Print a copy of the *Short Vowel Exemplar.kid* template shown below. Place the printed version in the center; instruct students on how to self-check their work.

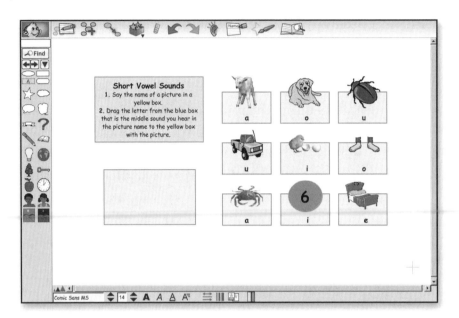

- Rather than using teacher-selected symbols when demonstrating the skill as explained in #3 under Instructions, the teacher may elect to use another consonant-vowel-consonant activity from **Kidspiration 3 Teacher menu> Teacher Resources Online>Lesson Plans** to teach the lesson.

- The activity may be used in Guided Reading groups with students who need additional experience with matching letters and vowel sounds.

English Language Learners

This lesson will help English language learners to become aware of the role of vowels in words. Students will need to know the names of the pictures prior to completing the activity, as well as the words *vowel* and *consonant*. In a small group prior to teaching the lesson, teach and/or review the names of the pictures used in the activity. Say the name of the picture and have students repeat it.

Spelling Patterns

Standards

✦ McREL Standards – Language Arts

(http://www.mcrel.org/standards-benchmarks/)

- Uses the general skills and strategies of the reading process
- Uses basic elements of phonetic analysis

✦ Grade Levels: K-2 (Ages 5-8)

Description

Phonics is the relationship between phonemes (sounds) and graphemes (letters/spellings that represent sounds). It is how the sounds of speech are represented by letters; students use the rules of phonics to read and write. Phonics includes an array of graphophonemic skills, including the knowledge of phonograms. In addition to helping students improve comprehension and organize ideas for writing, Kidspiration® can be used as a tool to help students learn, practice and apply specific phonics skills, supporting the teacher's reading curriculum.

Phonograms are the rimes, or the last parts of words. They are often referred to as spelling patterns or word families. When students are aware of and generalize the use of spelling patterns, they provide a significant resource for expanding reading and writing vocabularies. Additionally, once aware of spelling patterns, students will begin to notice them independently. In this Kidspiration activity, students will build words based on spelling patterns and their knowledge of letter sounds.

Note: This lesson is suitable for students who have knowledge of consonant digraphs and blends. At the teacher's discretion, use the term *word pattern* or *word family* to teach the lesson.

Instructions

1. Prior to beginning the lesson, read aloud a book that emphasizes vowel sounds and rhymes. Suggestions are: *Ten Little Bears* by Kathleen Hague or *Mama Zooms* by Jane Gowen-Fletcher. After reading the selection, share with students that they will use the sounds and patterns of rhyming words today, just like the author did in the book, to help them read and write words.

2. Go to **Kidspiration 3 Teacher menu>Teacher Resources Online>Lesson Plans** and open the *Spelling Patterns Exemplar.kid* activity, shown below.

Share with students that they have been learning a lot about letters and how they form words. Point to the words in the columns. Ask students to look carefully at how the words are sorted. Ask, "How are the words in each column the same?" Guide the students in responding that the ending of the words in each column are the same. As a class, read the words in each column.

3. Point to the words in one of the columns in random order. As the word is selected, read the word together or call upon a student to read the word aloud to the class. Point out that knowing that the ending of the words was the same made reading the words easier. Explain that recognizing patterns in words will help them to read and write words more easily.

4. Point out to students that some of the beginning letters in the activity could make real words in either column. Demonstrate using the letter *l*, placing it in both columns forming the words *lap* and *law*. Explain that it is up to them to decide in which column to place it. Also, explain that they may have letters left in the pink box. This is fine. The purpose is to use all the letters they can to make real words.

5. After directions have been given, allow students to complete the activity independently using the *Spelling Patterns.kia* activity shown below.

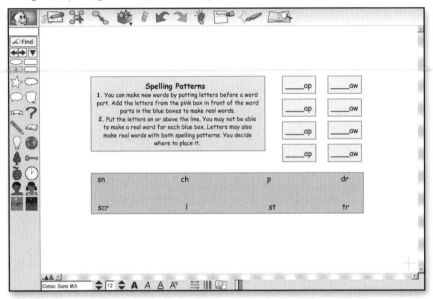

Additional phonics activities can be located here: **Kidspiration 3 Teacher menu>Teacher Resources Online>Lesson Plans.**

Assessment

- Confirm that students have completed the activity, matching beginning letters to word patterns that form real words.

- Observe if students use spelling patterns in their writing.

- Observe if students use spelling patterns to self-monitor when reading.

Adaptations

- The activity may be printed after its completion and used as an informal assessment.

- The activity may be used in a literacy center. Print copies of *Spelling Patterns Exemplar.kid*, making sure to include all possible combinations of letters and word patterns. Place the printed version in the center; instruct students on how to self-check their work.

English Language Learners

Students will be able to quickly expand their knowledge of word patterns. Ensure that students are able to read and understand all the words used in the lesson. Support students in talking about the patterns they are using and what they notice about the patterns.

Identifying Phonograms

Standards

✦ McREL Standards – Language Arts

(http://www.mcrel.org/standards-benchmarks/)

- Uses the general skills and strategies of the reading process
- Uses basic elements of phonetic analysis

✦ Grade Levels: K-2 (Ages 5-8)

Description

Phonics is the relationship between phonemes (sounds) and graphemes (letters/spellings that represent sounds). It is how the sounds of speech are represented by letters; students use the rules of phonics to read and write. Phonics includes an array of graphophonemic skills, including knowledge of phonograms. In addition to helping students improve comprehension and organize ideas for writing, Kidspiration® can be used as a tool to help students learn, practice and apply specific phonics skills, supporting the teacher's reading curriculum.

Phonograms are the rimes, or the last parts of words. Phonograms are also referred to as spelling patterns or word families. When students are aware of and generalize the use of phonograms, they provide a significant resource for expanding reading and writing vocabularies. Additionally, once aware of phonograms, students will begin to notice them independently. In this Kidspiration activity, students will sort words based on phonograms or word patterns.

Note: This lesson is suitable for students who have knowledge of short vowel sounds.

Instructions

1. Prior to beginning the lesson, read aloud a book that emphasizes vowel sounds and rhymes. Suggestions are: *Ten Little Bears* by Kathleen Hague or *Mama Zooms* by Jane Gowen-Fletcher. After reading the selection, share with students that they will use the sounds and patterns of words today, just like the author did in the book, and it will help them to read and write words.

2. Go to **Kidspiration 3 Teacher menu>Teacher Resources Online>Lesson Plans** and open the *Say and Sort.kia* activity, shown below.

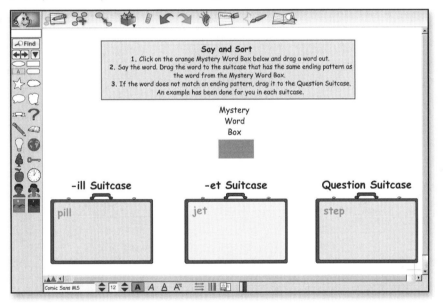

Share with students that they have been learning a lot about letters and how they form words, and today they're going to look at the ending parts in words.

3. Ask the students to read the words in the *–ill* and *–et* suitcases with you. Drag the first word, *let*, from the Mystery Word Box. Explain that the word is *let*. Instruct students to look at the ending part of the word. Ask which word in the activity is like *let*? Point out that the word *jet* and *let* have the same ending part or same ending pattern.

4. Demonstrate in the same manner using the next word in the Mystery Word Box, *hill*. Explain that recognizing patterns in words will help them to read and write words.

5. Drag the third word from the Mystery Word Box, *plan*. Lead students to discover that this word does not have the same ending part or pattern as do *let* and *hill*. Explain that because

this word does not have the same ending pattern as the other words, you will place it in the *Question Suitcase*.

6. Depending on students' grasp of the concept, the teacher should decide when to end modeling the skill. Students may then complete the activity independently. Encourage students to use their knowledge of ending parts when they read and write.

Additional phonics activities can be located here: **Kidspiration 3 Teacher menu>Teacher Resources Online>Lesson Plans.**

Assessment

- Confirm that students have completed the activity, sorting the words by ending patterns correctly.

- Observe if students use the ending patterns in their writing.

- Observe if students use the ending patterns to self-monitor when reading.

Adaptations

- The activity may be printed after its completion and used as an informal assessment.

- The activity may be used in a literacy center. Print a copy of the *Say and Sort Exemplar.kid* activity shown below. Place the printed version in the center; instruct students on how to self-check their work.

Say and Sort
1. Click on the orange Mystery Word Box below and drag a word out.
2. Say the word. Drag the word to the suitcase that has the same ending pattern as the word from the Mystery Word Box.
3. If the word does not match an ending pattern, drag it to the Question Suitcase. An example has been done for you in each suitcase.

Mystery
Word
Box

-ill Suitcase

| pill | hill | spill |
| mill | drill | quill |

-et Suitcase

| jet | let | fret |
| met | set | net |

Question Suitcase

| step | plan | rat |
| tend | sled | |

- During small-group instruction, have students build and sort other words that use the ending patterns of *–et* and *–ill* or use other common phonograms.

English Language Learners

English language learners will be able to quickly expand their knowledge and use of word patterns. Ensure that they are able to read and understand all the words used in the lesson. Support them in talking about the patterns they are using and what they notice about the patterns.

Recognizing Color Words

Standards

✴ McREL Standards – Language Arts

(http://www.mcrel.org/standards-benchmarks/)

- Uses the general skills and strategies of the reading process
- Uses basic elements of phonetic analysis
- Understands level-appropriate sight words and vocabulary

✴ Grade Levels: K-2 (Ages 5-8)

Description

Vocabulary knowledge is the ability to remember and utilize word meanings and pronunciations. Vocabulary skills include use of word structures, synonyms, antonyms, compound words and contextual clues, and reading high frequency words. Students learn vocabulary through wide-reading as well as direct instruction. In addition to helping students improve comprehension and organize ideas for writing, Kidspiration® can be used as a tool to help students learn and apply vocabulary skills, supporting the teacher's reading curriculum.

Related to vocabulary instruction there are two principles essentially agreed upon: the relationship between vocabulary and reading comprehension is significant, and poor vocabulary is detrimental to the academic success of students. For disadvantaged students especially, vocabulary deficiency is primary in accounting for academic failure. High frequency words, also known as sight vocabulary, are words students see many times as they read. This Kidspiration lesson will support learning to read color words by associating color with the word.

Instructions

1. Read Eric Carle's book, *Brown Bear, Brown Bear,* or *I Went Walking* by Sue Williams. Talk about the use of color words in the text and the pictorial support provided to help the reader read the text.

2. Explain to students that they will see some words many times when reading. Explain that today they will learn color words, some of them the same as the color words they just read in the book.

3. Go to **Kidspiration 3 Teacher menu>Teacher Resources Online>Lesson Plans** and open the *Color Words a.kia* activity, shown below.

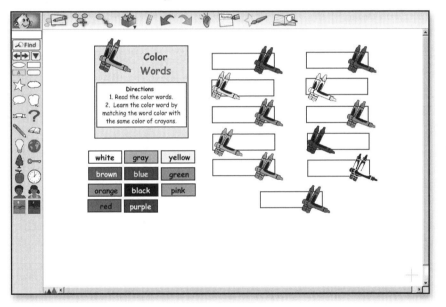

4. Explain to students that the symbols containing the color words match the color of the crayons. As students learn to read the color words, they can use the color in the activity. Remind them to use what they know about the sounds of letters in words as they read.

5. Demonstrate how to match the color word to its corresponding crayons, as well as using letter/sound knowledge when reading the color words.

6. After modeling the above, students may complete the activity independently. Depending on student ability, the teacher may elect to have students use the *Color Words b.kia* activity shown below. This activity mirrors the *Color Words a.kia* activity, without the support of the colored word symbols.

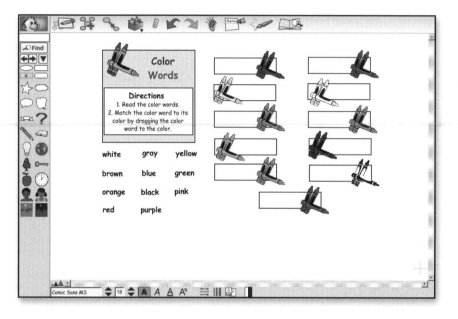

Additional vocabulary activities can be located here: **Kidspiration 3 Teacher menu>Teacher Resources Online>Lesson Plans.**

Assessment

- Confirm that students have completed the activity, matching the color words to the correct crayons.

- Observe if students use letter/sound knowledge as they read the color words.

Adaptations

- The activity may be printed after its completion and used as an informal assessment.

- The activity may be used in a literacy center. Print copies of the *Color Words Exemplar a.kid* activity and/or the *Color Words Exemplar b.kid* activity, shown below. Place the printed version in the center; instruct students on how to self-check their work.

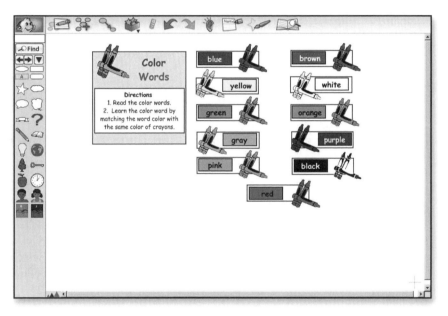

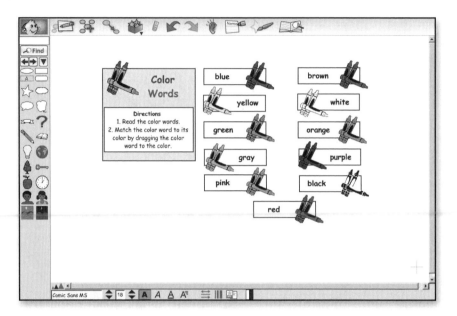

- Students can be asked to go to **Writing View**, and write a sentence using each color word. Students may be asked to write "I See" sentences using items located in the classroom. For example, *I see a brown bookcase.*

- As a class or independently, open Kidspiration to **Picture View** and use symbols and words to prewrite a book similar to Eric Carle's or Sue Williams'. After prewriting, switch to **Writing View** and write the text, using the color words learned in the *Color Words* activities. Print the text and have students illustrate the book.

English Language Learners

When possible, have students associate the color words in English with the color words in their native language. Consider having the English language learners teach the color words in their native language to the English-only students.

Matching Synonyms

Standards

✦ McREL Standards – Language Arts

(http://www.mcrel.org/standards-benchmarks/)

- Uses the general skills and strategies of the reading process
- Uses basic elements of phonetic analysis
- Understands level-appropriate sight words and vocabulary

✦ Grade Levels: K-2 (Ages 5-8)

Description

Vocabulary knowledge is the ability to remember and utilize word meanings and pronunciations. Vocabulary skills include use of word structures, synonyms, antonyms, compound words and contextual clues, and reading high frequency words. In addition to helping students improve comprehension and organize ideas for writing, Kidspiration® can be used as a tool to help students learn and apply vocabulary skills, supporting the teacher's reading curriculum.

Related to vocabulary instruction there are two principles essentially agreed upon: the relationship between vocabulary and reading comprehension is significant, and poor vocabulary is detrimental to the academic success of students. For disadvantaged students especially, vocabulary deficiency is primary in accounting for academic failure. With regards to synonyms, when students know that words can have the same or similar meanings, it helps them to associate words by meaning. Synonyms also help students make their writing more interesting, allowing them to select words that match the intended connotation. This Kidspiration lesson will support learning to read synonyms and the matching of words with similar meanings.

Instructions

1. Prior to the lesson, read aloud a book which emphasizes similarities and differences, pointing out the synonyms in the book as they are read. Suggestions are: *A Huge Hog is a Big Pig* by Francis McCall or *A Big Fat Enormous Lie* by Marjorie Sharmat.

2. Explain to students that some words mean about the same thing. These words are called *synonyms*. Today they are going to learn more about synonyms and like the author of the book just read, learn that synonyms can improve their writing.

3. Go to **Kidspiration 3 Teacher menu>Teacher Resources Online>Lesson Plans** and open the *Matching Synonyms.kia* activity, shown below.

4. Match the following words by dragging them to a purple box: *mend-repair, mean-cruel, odor-smell.* Ask students what they notice about the pairs of words. After they identify that they mean about the same thing, share that these pairs of words are called *synonyms*. Have the students say the word *synonym* with you.

5. Explain that today they will match pairs of synonyms using the activity as was just modeled. Demonstrate for students how to use the **Listen** tool should they not be able to independently read a word.

6. Read the directions together. If students are unfamiliar with the Kidspiration **Word Guide**, demonstrate its use. Once the directions are understood, have students complete the activity independently. Encourage students to use the **Word Guide** when writing to locate synonyms to make their writing more interesting.

Additional vocabulary activities can be located here: **Kidspiration 3 Teacher menu>Teacher Resources Online>Lesson Plans.**

Assessment

- Confirm that students have completed the activity, matching the pairs of synonyms correctly.

- Students should have used the **Word Guide** to add additional synonyms to the pairs in **Writing View**.

Adaptations

- The activity may be printed after its completion and used as an informal assessment.

- The activity may be used in a literacy center. Print a copy of the *Matching Synonyms Exemplar.kid* activity shown below. Place the printed version in the center; instruct students on how to self-check their work.

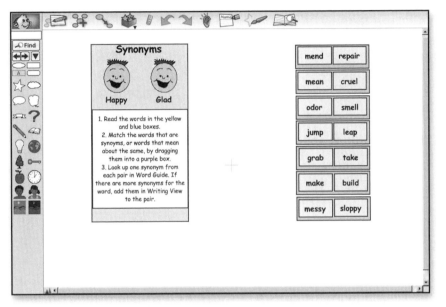

- Students can be asked to go to **Writing View**, and write a sentence using one of the synonyms from each group.

- As a class or independently, open Kidspiration to **Picture View**, and use symbols and words to pre-write a synonym book. Switch to **Writing View** and use the synonyms in sentences. Write the synonyms in a different font or font color. Print the book and have students illustrate the text if desired.

English Language Learners

Students will need to understand the meaning of both words in the synonym pairs. Assist students in understanding the words, pre-teaching the meaning in a small group if necessary. Once students understand the concept of synonyms, the use of the **Word Guide** to locate synonyms (and antonyms) will support expanding their vocabulary.

Building Compound Words

Standards

✸ McREL Standards – Language Arts

(http://www.mcrel.org/standards-benchmarks/)

- Uses the general skills and strategies of the reading process
- Uses basic elements of phonetic analysis
- Understands level-appropriate sight words and vocabulary
- Uses basic elements of structural analysis

✸ Grade Levels: K-2 (Ages 5-8)

Description

Vocabulary knowledge is the ability to remember and utilize word meanings and pronunciations. Vocabulary skills include use of word structures, synonyms, antonyms, compound words and contextual clues, and reading high frequency words. Students learn vocabulary through wide-reading as well as direct instruction. In addition to helping students improve comprehension and organize ideas for writing, Kidspiration® can be used as a tool to help students learn and apply vocabulary skills, supporting the teacher's reading curriculum.

Related to vocabulary instruction there are two principles essentially agreed upon: the relationship between vocabulary and reading comprehension is significant, and poor vocabulary is detrimental to the academic success of students. For disadvantaged students especially, vocabulary deficiency is primary in accounting for academic failure. Understanding word structures allows students to learn how words are related to one another and how words can be changed by adding letters, larger word parts or additional words. This Kidspiration lesson will support learning to combine words to make compound words.

Instructions

1. Prior to the lesson, read aloud *How Much Wood Could A Woodchuck Chuck?* by Danny Adlerman and Friends.

   Note: The final picture spread in this book depicts many compound words graphically. Explain to students that today they are going to learn about compound words.

2. Go to **Kidspiration 3 Teacher menu>Teacher Resources Online>Lesson Plans** and open the *Compound Words.kia* activity, shown below.

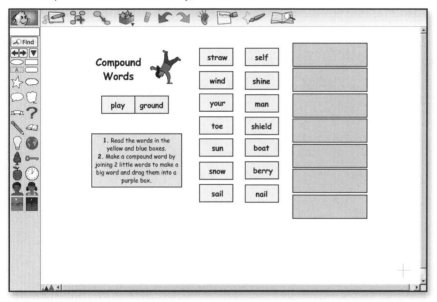

3. Explain to students that compound words are two little words joined together to make a new word. Also, often when reading we can read the "little words inside the big word" and it helps us read a word more easily. Match the following words by dragging them to a purple box while reading them aloud separately and then as a compound word: *straw-berry*, *wind-shield* and *your-self*. Discuss with students that each new word is made from two small words, but when the words are combined the new word has a different meaning than the two individual words. Share with them again that compound words are two little words joined together to make a new word. Have students say *compound word* with you.

4. Explain that they will join together two small words to make a compound word using this activity as was modeled for them. Demonstrate for students how to use the **Listen** tool should they not be able to independently read a word.

5. Read the directions together. Once the directions are understood, have students complete the activity independently.

Additional vocabulary activities can be located here: **Kidspiration 3 Teacher menu>Teacher Resources Online>Lesson Plans.**

Assessment

- Confirm that students have completed the activity, matching the words to make a compound word.

Adaptations

- The activity may be printed after its completion and used as an informal assessment.

- The activity may be used in a literacy center. Print a copy of the *Compound Words Exemplar.kid* activity shown below. Place the printed version in the center; instruct students on how to self-check their work.

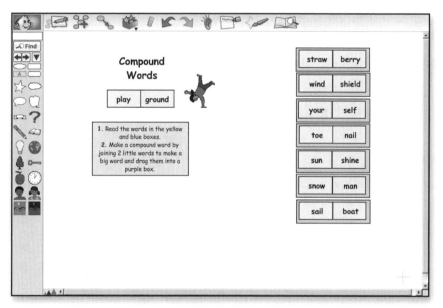

- Open Kidspiration in **Picture View**. Challenge students to use symbols from the **Symbol palette** or **Symbol Maker** to create compound words, e.g., symbol of a *dog* and a *house* to represent the compound word *doghouse*.

English Language Learners

Students will need to understand the meaning of both words in the compound word. Assist students in understanding the words, pre-teaching the meaning in a small group if necessary.

Understanding Contractions

Standards

✦ McREL Standards – Language Arts

(http://www.mcrel.org/standards-benchmarks/)

- Uses the general skills and strategies of the reading process
- Uses basic elements of phonetic analysis
- Understands level-appropriate sight words and vocabulary
- Uses basic elements of structural analysis

✦ Grade Levels: K-2 (Ages 5-8)

Description

Vocabulary knowledge is the ability to remember and utilize word meanings and pronunciations. Vocabulary skills include use of word structures, synonyms, antonyms, compound words and contextual clues, and reading high frequency words. Students learn vocabulary through wide-reading as well as direct instruction. In addition to helping students improve comprehension and organize ideas for writing, Kidspiration® can be used as a tool to help students learn and apply vocabulary skills, supporting the teacher's reading curriculum.

Related to vocabulary instruction there are two principles essentially agreed upon: the relationship between vocabulary and reading comprehension is significant, and poor vocabulary is detrimental to the academic success of students. For disadvantaged students especially, vocabulary deficiency is primary in accounting for academic failure. Students use contractions frequently in their daily speech. They use contractions in their writing and see them often in lower-leveled text. When students understand how contractions are formed, what they mean and how they are used, this understanding promotes correct use grammatically and with regards to the mechanics of writing. This Kidspiration lesson will support learning the conventions and meanings of contractions.

Instructions

1. Write on chart paper Judith Viorst's poem, "If I Were in Charge of the World" from *If I Were in Charge of the World and Other Worries, Poems for Children and their Parents*. Highlight the contractions in the poem. Read the poem to the students.

   Note: A different short text with contractions containing *not* and *would* may be used. Though this lesson focuses on contractions containing *not* and *would*, activities containing other contractions can be located here: **Kidspiration 3 Teacher menu>Teacher Resources Online>Lesson Plans.**

2. Ask students what they notice about the highlighted words. Confirm that students are noting the apostrophes in the contractions. Explain that each highlighted word is a contraction. A contraction is one word made of two words. A letter or letters are left out and an apostrophe is put in place of the letter or letters. Point to and name the apostrophe. Have the students say *apostrophe* with you.

3. Create a new Kidspiration activity in **Picture View**. Write the highlighted contractions from the poem on the activity. Draw the students' attention to the apostrophe in each contraction. Explain again that a contraction is one word made of two words. A letter or letters are left out of the word and an apostrophe is put in place of the letter or letters. Highlight a contraction on the activity and write the two words that make up the contraction below it. An example of the activity described is shown below.

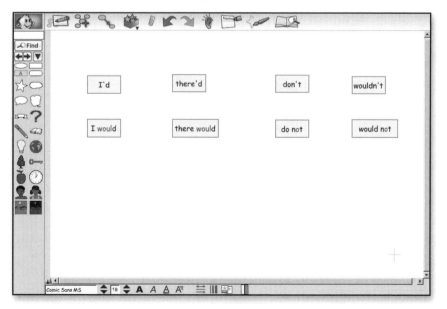

Ask the students to read the two words aloud. Ask students to tell you which letter or letters were left out when the apostrophe was added. Highlight the letter or letters left out using a different font or different text color.

4. Refer back to the poem and locate the contraction which was discussed above. Write the two words that formed the contraction on a yellow sticky note, placing it over the contraction on the chart paper. Follow the same procedure with each remaining contraction.

5. Re-read the entire poem, using the words written on the yellow sticky notes. Remove the yellow sticky notes, rereading the poem with its original contractions. Ask students if the poem still made sense even though it sounded a little different.

6. Go to **Kidspiration 3 Teacher menu>Teacher Resources Online>Lesson Plans** and open the *Contractions.kia* activity, shown below.

7. Explain to students that they will use what they have learned about contractions to complete the activity. They will drag the two words that make a contraction to the purple box. Demonstrate using the first contraction in the two left-hand columns.

8. Read the directions together. Once the directions are understood, have students complete the activity independently.

✓ Assessment

- Confirm that students have completed the activity, matching the two correct words with the contraction.

Adaptations

- The activity may be printed after its completion and used as an informal assessment.
- The activity may be used in a literacy center. Print a copy of the *Contractions Exemplar.kid* activity shown below. Place the printed version in the center; instruct students on how to self-check their work.

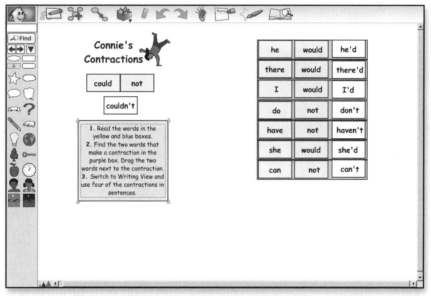

- Students can be asked to go to **Writing View**, and write a sentence using contractions in the activity.
- As a class or independently, open Kidspiration to **Picture View**, and use symbols and words to pre-write a different version of Judith Viorst's poem. Switch to **Writing View** and finish writing the poem. Print the poem. Poems may be collectively assembled into a class-published book, displayed in the classroom, read to classmates, etc.

English Language Learners

Contractions may be a new word structure for some students. If you know of similar structures in their native language, use those to help explain the concept. Additional small-group instruction may be needed in addition to using contractions in shorter sentence structures.

Recognizing Sight Words

Standards

✦ McREL Standards – Language Arts

(http://www.mcrel.org/standards-benchmarks/)

- Uses the general skills and strategies of the reading process
- Uses basic elements of phonetic analysis
- Understands level-appropriate sight words and vocabulary

✦ Grade Levels: K-2 (Ages 5-8)

Description

Vocabulary knowledge is the ability to remember and utilize word meanings and pronunciations. Vocabulary skills include use of word structures, synonyms, antonyms, compound words and contextual clues, and reading high frequency words. Students learn vocabulary through wide-reading as well as direct instruction. In addition to helping students improve comprehension and organize ideas for writing, Kidspiration® can be used as a tool to help students learn and apply vocabulary skills, supporting the teacher's reading curriculum.

Related to vocabulary instruction there are two principles essentially agreed upon: the relationship between vocabulary and reading comprehension is significant, and poor vocabulary is detrimental to the academic success of students. For disadvantaged students especially, vocabulary deficiency is primary in accounting for academic failure. A sight word, or high frequency, vocabulary is essential for young readers. Sight vocabulary words are a significant resource and support to students. It allows students to become automatic in their reading, improving decoding as well as comprehension. Students use their knowledge of sight words to self-check the accuracy of their reading as well as to read other unknown words, e.g., *they* starts like *the*. A sight word vocabulary also helps students to read beginning text and practice beginning reading behaviors. This Kidspiration activity will support students in learning to read sight words.

Instructions

1. Prior to the lesson, read aloud a book which contains a significant number of sight vocabulary words. Suggestions are: *Where's Spot* by Eric Carle or *Nuts to You* by Lois Ehlert. If possible, locate a text with large print. Call attention to the sight words in the text.

    Note: For this lesson, it is suggested that students have access to letter tiles or letter cards, one set per child. If letter tiles are not available, students should have access to paper and a pencil.

2. Explain to students that some words are seen many times when reading, just like some of the words in the book just read. These words are called *sight words*. Words that are seen many times, i.e., sight words, are important to know because they help us read and write.

3. Create a new Kidspiration activity in **Picture View**. Add the word *and* to the activity. Select a new font and write the word again in a new column to the right of the first. Again, change font and/or color of font and write *and* in a third column. An example of the activity described is shown below.

Ask students what they notice about the word. Responses should include it starts with an *a*, has 3 letters, etc. Instruct the students to build the word with their letter tiles. (If letter tiles are not available, have students write the word on paper.) Follow the same procedure with the following words: *from, the, a, you, to.*

4. Explain that today they will use what they learned and practice reading sight words, i.e., words readers see all the time.

5. Go to **Kidspiration 3 Teacher menu>Teacher Resources Online>Lesson Plans** and open the *Sight Words.kia* activity, shown below.

Read the directions together. Demonstrate how to listen to a word by clicking on the speaker icon. Point out that students can click on the speaker icon as often as necessary. Once the directions are understood, have students complete the activity independently.

Additional vocabulary activities can be located here: **Kidspiration 3 Teacher menu>Teacher Resources Online>Lesson Plans.**

✓ Assessment

- Confirm that students have completed the activity, placing the sight words in the correct location.

Adaptations

- The activity may be printed after its completion and used as an informal assessment.

- The activity may be used in a literacy center. Print a copy of the *Sight Words Exemplar.kid* activity shown below. Place the printed version in the center; instruct students on how to self-check their work.

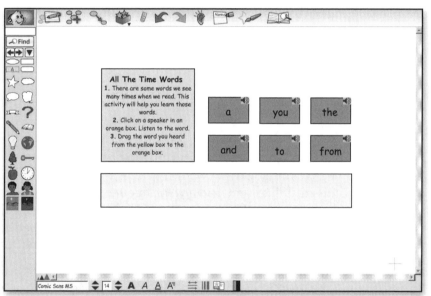

- Students can be asked to go to **Writing View**, and use each sight word in a sentence.

English Language Learners

A sight word vocabulary will help students attend to the details in words, which will help them remember the words when reading and writing. It will also help students connect their pronunciation to the sounds and letters. Students should be able to pronounce the words they are building with the letter tiles. Encourage students to attend to the details of each sight word, e.g., numbers of letters, beginning letter, etc.

Understanding Suffixes

Standards

✴ McREL Standards – Language Arts

(http://www.mcrel.org/standards-benchmarks/)

- Uses the general skills and strategies of the reading process
- Uses basic elements of phonetic analysis
- Uses basic elements of structural analysis

✴ Grade Levels: K-2 (Ages 5-8)

Description

Vocabulary knowledge is the ability to remember and utilize word meanings and pronunciations. Vocabulary skills include use of word structures, synonyms, antonyms, compound words and contextual clues, and reading high frequency words. Students learn vocabulary through wide-reading as well as direct instruction. In addition to helping students improve comprehension and organize ideas for writing, Kidspiration® can be used as a tool to help students learn and apply vocabulary skills, supporting the teacher's reading curriculum.

Related to vocabulary instruction there are two principles essentially agreed upon: the relationship between vocabulary and reading comprehension is significant, and poor vocabulary is detrimental to the academic success of students. For disadvantaged students especially, vocabulary deficiency is primary in accounting for academic failure. Affixes (suffixes and prefixes), when added to a base word (a complete word), have meaning associated with them. Understanding the meaning of affixes provides students with an additional resource related to vocabulary and comprehension. This Kidspiration lesson will support students in learning the meaning of the suffixes *–er* and *–ing* and their application within sentences.

Instructions

1. Read a book containing several words with the –*ing* suffix. Suggested titles are: *One Sunday Morning* by Yumi Heo or *Iron Horses* by Verla Kay. Point out the words containing the –*ing* suffix.

2. Explain to students that the words pointed out in the story had –*ing* added to the base words. The –*ing* ending is called a *suffix*. Today they are going to learn about two suffixes, -*ing* and –*er*. Suffixes, when added to a base word, change the meaning of the base word. Knowing the meaning of suffixes can help them understand new words.

3. Create a new Kidspiration activity in **Picture View**. From the *School > Arts* library select a *dancer* and the *painter* symbol, placing them on the activity. From the *School > Sports* library, select the *swimmer, skier* and *surfer*, placing them on the activity also.

4. Share with the students that the suffix –*er* when added to a base word, means *a person that does something*. Click on the symbol of the *dancer*. Explain that a person who dances is a dancer. Write *dancer* under the symbol and verbally use the word in a sentence. An example of the activity is shown below.

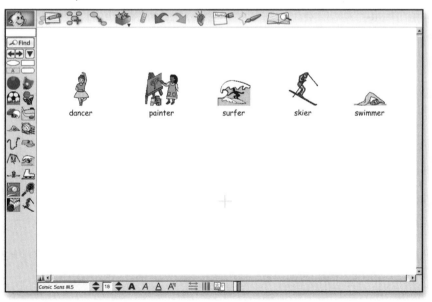

Continue in the same manner using the remainder of the symbols, gradually moving from demonstration for students to guided practice by the students.

5. Next explain that when the suffix *–ing* is added to a word, it makes the word *a verb* and *shows action*. Copy the symbol of the *surfer* and place it under the word *surfer*. Delete the word *surfer* and replace it with the word *surf*. Explain that when *–ing* is added to the word *surf*, the word becomes a verb and shows action. The action is surfing. Add *–ing* to the word *surf* and verbally use the word in a sentence. Continue in the same manner using the remainder of the symbols, gradually moving from demonstration for students to guided practice by the students.

6. Go to **Kidspiration 3 Teacher menu>Teacher Resources Online>Lesson Plans** and open the *Suffixes. kia* activity, shown below.

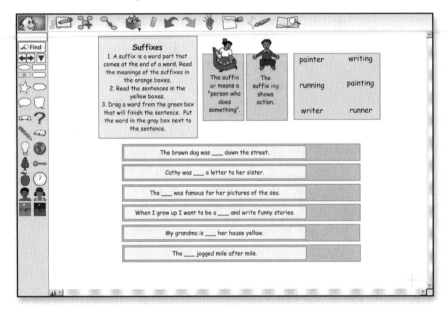

Share with students that they will now use what they learned about the suffixes *–er* and *-ing* to complete the activity. Read the directions together. Remind students that knowing what suffixes mean and how they change the meaning of words will help them understand new words when they read. Once the directions are understood, have students complete the activity independently.

Additional vocabulary activities can be located here: **Kidspiration 3 Teacher menu>Teacher Resources Online>Lesson Plans.**

Assessment

- Confirm that students have completed the activity, matching the words with the correct sentences.

Adaptations

- The activity may be printed after its completion and used as an informal assessment.

- The activity may be used in a literacy center. Print a copy of the *Suffixes Exemplar.kid* activity shown below. Place the printed version in the center; instruct students on how to self-check their work.

Suffixes

1. A suffix is a word part that comes at the end of a word. Read the meanings of the suffixes in the orange boxes.
2. Read the sentences in the yellow boxes.
3. Drag a word from the green box that will finish the sentence. Put the word in the gray box next to the sentence.

The suffix er means a "person who does something".

The suffix ing shows action.

The brown dog was ___ down the street.	running
Cathy was ___ a letter to her sister.	writing
The ___ was famous for her pictures of the sea.	painter
When I grow up I want to be a ___ and write funny stories.	writer
My grandma is ___ her house yellow.	painting
The ___ jogged mile after mile.	runner

- Students can be asked to go to **Writing View**, and use each word in a new sentence.

English Language Learners

Word endings such as suffixes can be challenging to English language learners because the syntax has yet to be internalized. Students need many opportunities to encounter simple sentences using words which contain suffixes. In small groups, construct simple sentences using known concepts to allow students to interact with the syntax. When saying the words which contain the suffix, segment it slightly, calling attention to the suffix.

Content Vocabulary, ABC Pranks

Standards

✴ McREL Standards – Language Arts

(http://www.mcrel.org/standards-benchmarks/)

- Uses the general skills and strategies of the reading process
- Understands level-appropriate sight words and vocabulary
- Uses basic elements of phonetic analysis

✴ Grade Levels: K-2 (Ages 5-8)

Description

Vocabulary knowledge is the ability to remember and utilize word meanings and pronunciations. Vocabulary skills include use of word structures, synonyms, antonyms, compound words and contextual clues, and reading high frequency words. Students learn vocabulary through wide-reading as well as direct instruction. In addition to helping students improve comprehension and organize ideas for writing, Kidspiration® can be used as a tool to help students learn and apply vocabulary skills, supporting the teacher's reading curriculum.

Related to vocabulary instruction there are two principles essentially agreed upon: the relationship between vocabulary and reading comprehension is significant, and poor vocabulary is detrimental to the academic success of students. For disadvantaged students especially, vocabulary deficiency is primary in accounting for academic failure. Though no single approach to vocabulary instruction is most effective, active student engagement is key. This Kidspiration activity encourages students to become active learners as they make connections between words, concepts, and graphical representations of new words, thus providing visual and textual support.

Instructions

1. Discuss with students how important it is as readers to remember what new vocabulary means so we can understand the author's message. Explain that today they will learn to use an activity that will help them remember new vocabulary words, which will help them understand what they have read. Read a grade appropriate expository text, related to a current unit of study.

2. Go to **Kidspiration 3 Teacher menu>Teacher Resources Online>Lesson Plans** and open the *ABC Pranks Exemplar.kid* activity, shown below, and review it with students.

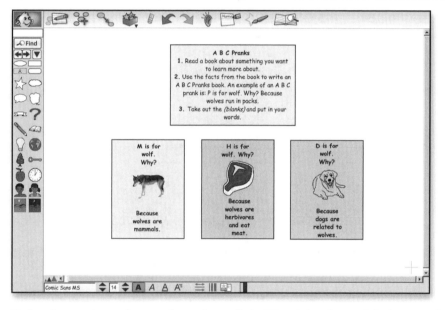

Define for students the word *prank* as a "*joke.*" Read the three alphabet prank cards to the students. Ask students to predict why this activity is called "ABC Pranks."

3. Explain to students that as learners we more easily remember new words when we are having fun learning and when we are linking them to our background knowledge, i.e., to what we already know. Share that they will use this fun and creative activity to learn and remember new vocabulary associated with units of study.

4. Close the *ABC Pranks Exemplar.kid* activity and create a new Kidspiration activity in **Picture View**. Brainstorm facts learned from the book read at the beginning of the lesson. As a class, generate the *ABC pranks* to be used in the *ABC Pranks* activity. Once the ideas are generated, save the brainstorming activity and open the *ABC Pranks.kia* activity, shown below. Complete the three symbols with the class-generated *ABC pranks*.

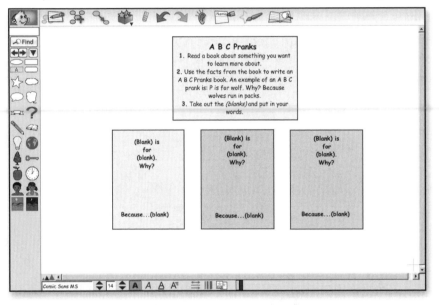

5. At this point, the teacher may decide to complete additional *ABC Pranks* as a class, using additional activities, or have students complete the activity independently.

6. Should the students continue independently, review the directions with them. Remind students that today they learned to use an activity that helps them remember new words. As readers, it's important to be able to remember the meaning of words in order to understand the author's message.

   Note: If students are to complete the activity using a book other than the book the teacher read at the beginning of the lesson, the students' books should be at their independent reading level.

Additional vocabulary activities can be located here: **Kidspiration 3 Teacher menu>Teacher Resources Online>Lesson Plans**.

Assessment

- Confirm that students have completed the activity as instructed, and words and pictorial representations of the vocabulary words are appropriate.

 ## Adaptations

- Several activities can be utilized for a unit of study.

- Activities can be printed, cut apart and made into books.

- Depending on the content and purpose of the vocabulary study, students may self-select words to add to the activity.

- Students may be assigned specific page numbers from which to take the vocabulary words in order to complete the activity.

English Language Learners

English language learners may need additional support to understand the content within the text. Consider pre-teaching the vocabulary from the text in small groups prior to the lesson.

Plurals: Adding -es

Standards

✦ McREL Standards – Language Arts

(http://www.mcrel.org/standards-benchmarks/)

- Uses the general skills and strategies of the reading process
- Understands level-appropriate sight words and vocabulary
- Uses basic elements of phonetic analysis

✦ Grade Levels: K-2 (Ages 5-8)

Description

Vocabulary knowledge is the ability to remember and utilize word meanings and pronunciations. Vocabulary skills include use of word structures, synonyms, antonyms, compound words and contextual clues, and reading high frequency words. Students learn vocabulary through wide-reading as well as direct instruction. In addition to helping students improve comprehension and organize ideas for writing, Kidspiration® can be used as a tool to help students learn and apply vocabulary skills, supporting the teacher's reading curriculum.

Related to vocabulary instruction there are two principles essentially agreed upon: the relationship between vocabulary and reading comprehension is significant, and poor vocabulary is detrimental to the academic success of students. For disadvantaged students especially, vocabulary deficiency is primary in accounting for academic failure. Students need to understand there are different ways of forming the plurals of words. This Kidspiration lesson will support students in learning when to add *–es* to make a word plural.

Note: This lesson is appropriate for students who have worked with adding *–s* to form plurals. Students should also able to clap the number of syllables in words.

Instructions

1. Read a book containing plurals. Suggested titles are: *One Moose, Twenty Mice* by Clare Beaton or *Toby Counts His Marbles* by Cyndy Szekeres. Point out the plurals formed with –*s* and –*es*.

2. Explain to students that the words pointed out in the story were *plurals. Plural means more than one.* Tell students that they already know about making plurals by adding -*s*; today they will learn about making plurals by adding -*es*.

3. Create a new Kidspiration activity in **Picture View**. From the *Transportation* library in the **Symbol palette**, select the *bus* symbol and place it on the activity. Ask the students what the picture shows. Write *bus* under the symbol. Add another *bus* symbol to the activity. Say to the children, "Now what do I have? Yes, buses. Think about what I'm doing as I write the word buses. Here is another one, peach." Add a *peach* symbol from the *Food & Health>Fruits & Veggies* library and place it on the activity. Follow the same procedure as used for the word *bus*. Continue in the same manner using the following symbols: *kiss, church, dish*. You can demonstrate performing a **Symbol Search** in order to find these additional symbols. An example of the activity described is shown below.

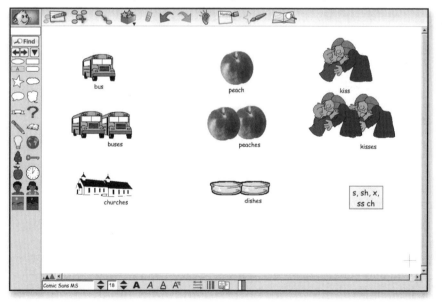

4. Explain to students that they can hear the –*es* at the end of the words. Have students read the words with you. Some students may notice that the –*es* sounds like a *z*.

5. Share with the students that they can also hear the word parts. Have students clap *bus*, and ask how many word parts it had. Then have students clap the word *buses*, again asking how many parts it had. Continue with the other words on the activity in the same manner, helping the students understand that plurals that end in *–es* have two word parts.

6. Next explain that when words end with *s, sh, x, ss* or *ch* we need to add *–es* to make the word plural. Add a rectangle symbol to the activity and write the above word endings inside the symbol.

7. Ask students what they learned about the words in the activity. Responses should include: words ending in *s, sh, x, ss* or *ch* need to have *–es* added to make the word plural, the words sound like they end with *z* and plural words ending in *–es* have two parts.

8. Now close the activity and open the *Plurals Adding -es.kia* activity shown below.

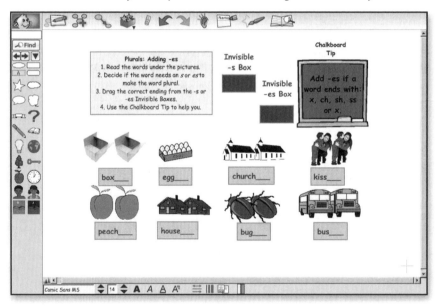

Share with students that they will now use what they learned about making words plural. Preview the activity, reading the directions together. Demonstrate how to pull a *–s* or *–es* from the *Invisible Boxes*, making sure students understand that they can't see the suffix until it's pulled from the box. Once directions are understood, have the students complete the activity independently.

Additional vocabulary activities can be located here: **Kidspiration 3 Teacher menu>Teacher Resources Online>Lesson Plans.**

Assessment

- Confirm that students have completed the activity, using the correct form to make the plural.

Adaptations

- The activity may be printed after its completion and used as an informal assessment.

- The activity may be used in a literacy center. Print a copy of the *Plural Adding –es Exemplar. Kid* activity shown below. Place the printed version in the center; instruct students on how to self-check their work.

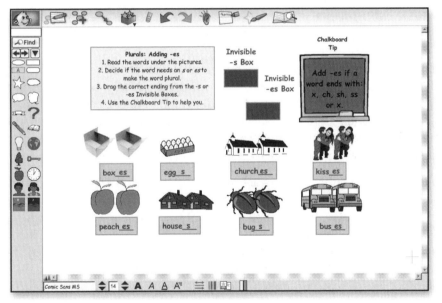

- Students can be asked to go to **Writing View**, and use each word in a sentence.

English Language Learners

It is important prior to this lesson that students have worked with forming simple plurals and they understand the concept of more than one. Make sure students are able to read the words and have them talk about what they notice about the words.

Word Map

Standards

✦ McREL Standards – Language Arts

(http://www.mcrel.org/standards-benchmarks/)

- Uses the general skills and strategies of the reading process
- Understands level-appropriate sight words and vocabulary

✦ Grade Levels: K-2 (Ages 5-8)

Description

Vocabulary knowledge is the ability to remember and utilize word meanings and pronunciations. Vocabulary skills include use of word structures, synonyms, antonyms, compound words and contextual clues, and reading high frequency words. Students learn vocabulary through wide-reading as well as direct instruction. In addition to helping students improve comprehension and organize ideas for writing, Kidspiration® can be used as a tool to help students learn and apply vocabulary skills, supporting the teacher's reading curriculum.

Related to vocabulary instruction there are two principles essentially agreed upon: the relationship between vocabulary and reading comprehension is significant, and poor vocabulary is detrimental to the academic success of students. For disadvantaged students especially, vocabulary deficiency is primary in accounting for academic failure. Though no single approach to vocabulary instruction is most effective, active student engagement is key. This Kidspiration activity encourages students to become active learners as they make connections between words, concepts, and graphical representations of new words, thus providing visual and textual support.

Instructions

1. Read an expository text related to a current unit of study which contains content-specific vocabulary. Discuss with students the importance of learning and remembering new vocabulary so we can understand the author's message. Explain that today they will learn to use an activity which will help them learn and remember new vocabulary words.

2. Open the *Word Map Exemplar.kid* activity, shown below, and review it with students. Explain that as learners we more easily remember new words when we can link them to our background knowledge, i.e., to what we already know. Further explain that a picture of a word is easily remembered and can help us remember what a word means. Share that they will use the *Word Map* activity to learn and remember new vocabulary associated with units of study.

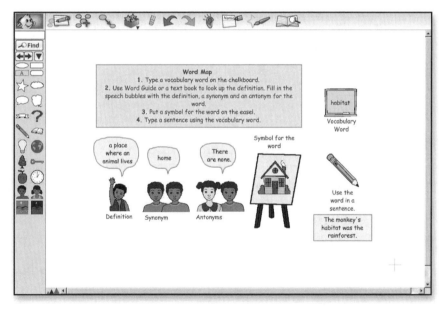

3. Demonstrate to students how to use the Kidspiration **Word Guide** and **Listen** tool. Explain that students may use the **Word Guide** to help them look up definitions and depending on the entry word, they may find synonyms and antonyms for the new vocabulary word. Additionally, demonstrate for students how to perform a **Symbol Search** feature to locate a symbol to represent the vocabulary word visually.

4. Go to **Kidspiration 3 Teacher menu>Teacher Resources Online>Lesson Plans** and open the *Word Map.kia* activity, shown below. Using a word from a current unit of study or from the content book read at the beginning of the lesson, model completing the activity.

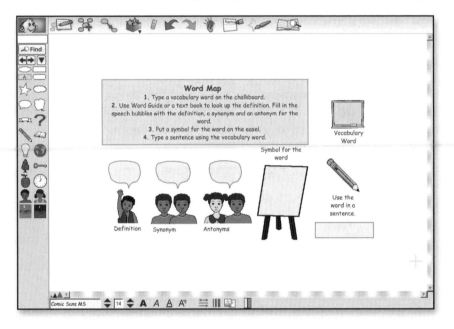

5. Review the directions in the activity. Remind students that it's important to be able to learn and remember the meaning of words to understand the author's message. Assign students vocabulary words and have them complete the activity independently.

Additional vocabulary activities can be located here: **Kidspiration 3 Teacher menu>Teacher Resources Online>Lesson Plans.**

Assessment

- Confirm that students have completed the activity as instructed and words and visual representations of the vocabulary words are appropriate.

Adaptations

- Several activities can be utilized for a unit of study.

- Activities can be printed and used as a study guide.

- Students can switch to **Writing View** and add additional information about the vocabulary word.

- Depending on the content and purpose of the vocabulary study, students may self-select words to add to the activity.

English Language Learners

Allow English language learners to use synonyms and antonyms from their native language if possible when completing the activity. This allows them to take full advantage of their background knowledge to learn new vocabulary.

Strategies for Reading Nonfiction

Standards

✴ McREL Standards – Language Arts

(http://www.mcrel.org/standards-benchmarks/)

- Uses reading skills and strategies to understand and interpret a variety of informational texts
- Understands the main idea and supporting details of simple expository information
- Summarizes information found in texts
- Relates new information to prior knowledge and experience

✴ Grade Levels: K-2 (Ages 5-8)

Description

Comprehension is the ability to understand, remember and communicate ideas read. Active readers use comprehension strategies to make sense of text. Strategies include: inferring, making connections, determining importance, summarizing, questioning and synthesizing information. Active readers use many strategies as they read. Prior to reading, they preview pictures and illustrations to activate background knowledge. During reading, active readers ask questions, establishing a purpose for reading. After reading, active readers confirm whether their questions were answered and summarize what they have learned. These reading skills and strategies help readers understand a variety of text. In this lesson, students will use a Kidspiration® activity to support the use of several strategies while reading nonfiction or expository text.

Instructions

1. Select a short informational book containing pictures and/or illustrations for this lesson.

2. Explain that active readers use many strategies before, during and after reading informational text. Today they will learn how to apply several of those strategies. Explain that active readers preview informational text to predict the text's content and connect their prior knowledge to the topic. Active readers also ask their own questions as they read, read to have the questions answered and summarize after reading what they learned. These strategies help readers remember what they have read.

3. Go to **Kidspiration 3 Teacher menu>Teacher Resources Online>Lesson Plans** and open the *Reading Nonfiction.kia* activity, shown below, and review it with students.

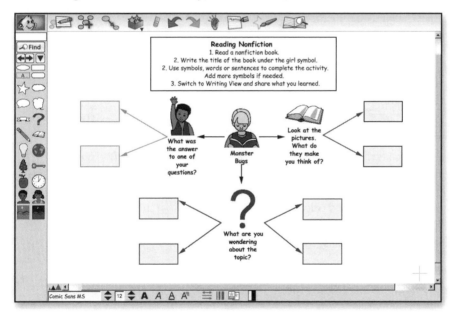

If you would like to view an exemplar prior to beginning the lesson, open the *Reading Nonfiction Exemplar.kid* template shown below.

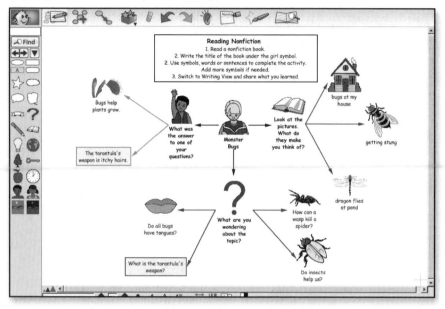

4. Use a "think-aloud" to model completing the activity. Begin by explaining that active readers preview the pictures and illustrations to activate their prior knowledge and to see what they will learn about while reading. Preview the pictures and illustrations in the text selected. Model asking questions prior to reading the text. Most initial questions will be associated with the pictures and illustrations that were previewed. Record questions from previewing in the appropriate symbols.

5. Begin to read the text, and continue to record questions during reading.

6. After reading the text, select two questions and record the answers to the questions.

7. Switch to **Writing View** and model summarizing what was learned.

   Note: You may determine the number of sentences to be included in the summary depending on students' abilities.

8. When students have had sufficient guided practice in completing the activity, have students complete an activity independently, reading text at their independent reading level. Prior to students doing the activity independently, remind students that active readers use many strategies as they read. Before reading, they preview pictures and illustrations to activate background knowledge and ask questions. During reading, active readers ask questions

and read to find the answers. After reading, active readers confirm whether their questions were answered and summarize what they have learned. Whenever they read, especially when reading nonfiction, students should use these strategies.

Assessment

- Confirm that connections between students' schema and the text's graphics are applicable to the content and reasonable.
- Questions should relate to the content of the text.
- Answers to the two questions should be correct.
- Evaluate the summary in **Writing View** for accuracy.

Adaptations

- When completing the activity independently, students should read books at their independent reading level.
- More than one activity may be used for a text.
- The summary written in **Writing View** may be printed and utilized as a simple report.
- The activity may be utilized with fictional text as well.

Retelling a Story

Standards

✴ McREL Standards – Language Arts

(http://www.mcrel.org/standards-benchmarks/)

- Uses reading skills and strategies to understand and interpret a variety of literary texts

- Knows the main ideas or theme of a story

✴ Grade Levels: K-2 (Ages 5-8)

Description

Comprehension is the ability to understand, remember and communicate ideas read. Active readers use comprehension strategies to make sense of text. Strategies include: inferring, making connections, determining importance, summarizing, questioning and synthesizing information. Young readers, often familiar with the structure of fiction, i.e., beginning, middle and end, benefit from using a graphic organizer to help them learn to retell or summarize a story. Retelling is synthesizing in its simplest form. This Kidspiration® lesson provides a framework from which students can synthesize information through a brief retell.

Instructions

1. Go to **Kidspiration 3 Teacher menu>Teacher Resources Online>Lesson Plans** and open the *Retelling a Story.kia* activity, shown below, and review it with students.

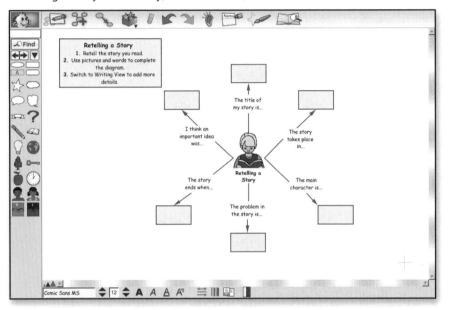

Explain the differences between fiction and expository texts and their structures, particularly that fictional structures include setting, characters, and a problem and a solution which occurs in the beginning, middle and end. Share that students will learn to use an activity, like a map, when retelling a story. When students retell, they share what was important in the story, retelling the story in a way that makes sense, and they are brief and don't share too much detail.

2. Prior to reading a fictional text selected for the lesson, remind students that the purpose of the reading is to be able to complete the reviewed activity to help them retell the story. A suggested story for this lesson is Robert Munsch's *Stephanie's Ponytail*. Its story structures are easily identifiable and the story is engaging.

3. Read the selected text.

4. Use a "think-aloud" to model completing the activity with information from the book.

   Note: If you would like to view an exemplar prior to modeling the lesson, review the *Retelling a Story Exemplar.kid* shown below. The activity below was completed using the story *Stephanie's Ponytail*.

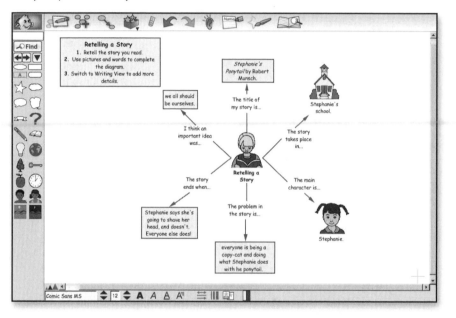

5. After modeling completing the activity, ask students to turn to a partner and take turns orally completing the retell.

6. After students have had sufficient guided practice in completing the activity to retell stories, students should be allowed to complete an activity independently, reading text at their independent reading level.

Additional comprehension lessons can be located here: **Kidspiration 3 Teacher menu>Teacher Resources Online>Lesson Plans.**

Assessment

- Confirm that students follow the activity, completing it with information from the text. Retelling should reveal an awareness of the text's content and contain accurate information.

Adaptations

- When the activity is completed independently, students should read books at their independent reading level.

- A copy of the activity may be printed and displayed in the classroom or in students' individual literacy folders, providing a reference for retelling other stories.

- The activity may be used as part of an informal running record and included in documentation for comprehension of the text. After the student has completed the activity, print a copy and attach the running record.

- A follow-up lesson on a story's theme may be taught using the "I think an important idea was…."

Nonfiction: Activating Prior Knowledge

Standards

✴ McREL Standards – Language Arts

(http://www.mcrel.org/standards-benchmarks/)

- Uses reading skills and strategies to understand and interpret a variety of informational texts
- Relates new information to prior knowledge and experience
- Uses meaning clues to aid comprehension and make predictions about content

✴ Grade Levels: K-2 (Ages 5-8)

Description

Comprehension is the ability to understand, remember and communicate ideas read. Active readers use comprehension strategies to make sense of text. Strategies include: inferring, making connections, determining importance, summarizing, questioning and synthesizing information. When active readers preview text, they make predictions about what they will learn and activate their prior knowledge about the topic. For young readers, having them predict what words will be seen in text allows them to do both simultaneously. This Kidspiration® activity supports young readers in making predictions and activating prior knowledge.

Instructions

1. Go to **Kidspiration 3 Teacher menu>Teacher Resources Online>Lesson Plans** and open the *Activating Prior Knowledge.kia* activity, shown below, and review it with students.

Share with students that active readers predict what they will see and learn before reading a new book. They also think about what they already know about a topic to help them learn new information. Explain that today they will use this activity to make predictions and activate their background knowledge, i.e., what they already know about the topic.

Note: Prior to teaching the lesson, if you would like to view an exemplar of the activity, open the *Prior Knowledge Exemplar.kid* shown below.

2. Preview the informational text selected for the lesson, making note of the cover, title, picture, graphs, etc.

3. Ask students to brainstorm a list of words they think will be seen and read in the text. As students present words to be added to the list, ask why they think the word will be in the text. Type predicted words into symbols located below *Words we predict to see as we read*.

4. Read the text to the students. Have them listen and look for the words on the list.

5. After the text is read, identify the words from the list that were included in the text. Drag the words read from the first column to the second column, *Words we saw as we read*.

6. Discuss why the words identified in step five were used in the text.

7. After students have had sufficient guided practice in completing the activity, students should be allowed to complete the activity independently, reading text at their independent reading level.

Additional comprehension lessons can be located here: **Kidspiration 3 Teacher menu>Teacher Resources Online>Lesson Plans.**

Assessment

- Confirm that students' word predictions make sense and are relevant to the topic. Students' word predictions should relate to their background knowledge and experiences with the topic.

- The words added to the *Words we saw as we read* should be words that were included in the text.

Adaptations

- This activity works well for a unit of study for younger students. As students learn more about the topic, the words predicted to be seen should indicate greater understanding of topic vocabulary. When using the activity at the onset of a unit, predicted words will provide information regarding the students' level of understanding about the topic.

- A discussion as to why words were not seen in the text may serve as a follow-up activity to the lesson.

- When the activity is completed independently, students should read books at their independent reading level.

Expository Text: Retell Framework

Standards

✸ McREL Standards – Language Arts

(http://www.mcrel.org/standards-benchmarks/)

- Uses reading skills and strategies to understand and interpret a variety of informational texts
- Summarizes information found in texts

✸ Grade Levels: K-2 (Ages 5-8)

Description

Comprehension is the ability to understand, remember and communicate ideas read. Active readers use comprehension strategies to make sense of text. Strategies include: inferring, making connections, determining importance, summarizing, questioning and synthesizing information. Active readers use many strategies as they read. Young readers, often familiar with the structure of fiction, i.e., beginning, middle and end, benefit from using a graphic organizer to help them learn to retell or summarize information from expository text. This Kidspiration® activity incorporates the gradual release of responsibility for learning from the teacher to student, beginning with demonstration and shared demonstration, and ending with independent practice in learning how to retell information from an expository text.

Instructions

1. Go to **Kidspiration 3 Teacher menu>Teacher Resources Online>Lesson Plans** and open the *Expository Text Retell.kia* activity, shown below, and review it with students. Explain the differences between fiction and expository texts and their structures. Point out that when reading expository text, the book does not have characters, setting, etc. The text doesn't tell a story; we learn things from reading expository text.

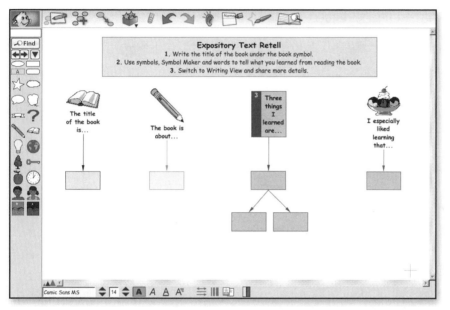

2. Select a high interest informational text. A title suggestion is *Cactus Hotel* by Brenda Z. Guiberson. Prior to reading the text selected for the lesson, remind students that the purpose of this reading is to be able to complete an activity to help them retell the information learned in the book.

3. Read the text.

4. Use a "think-aloud" to model completing the activity with information from the book.

   Note: If you would like to view an exemplar prior to modeling the lesson, review the *Expository Text Exemplar.kid* activity shown below.

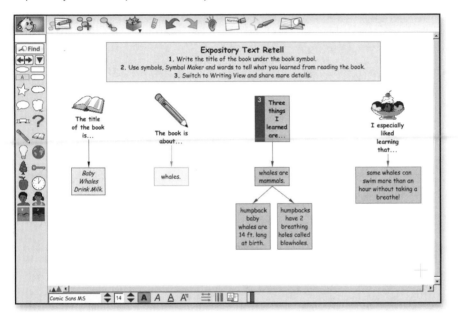

5. After completing the activity, ask students to turn to a partner and take turns orally completing the retell. Students may use the information the teacher used to complete the retell or add other information from the text.

6. After students have had sufficient guided practice in completing the activity to retell information from an expository text, students should be allowed to complete the activity independently, reading text at their independent reading level.

Additional comprehension lessons can be located here: **Kidspiration 3 Teacher menu>Teacher Resources Online>Lesson Plans.**

Assessment

- Confirm that students follow the activity, completing it with information from the text. Retelling should reveal an awareness of the text's content and contain accurate information.

Adaptations

- For text that contains chapters, an activity may be used for each chapter.

- After the activity is completed, students may switch to **Writing View** to generate a report. Teachers may elect to have students add additional information depending on the students' writing abilities.

- When completing the activity independently, students should read books at their independent reading level.

- To set a specific purpose for reading, a teacher may instruct students to attend to a specific part of the text or particular facts and content within the text. For example, if reading a book about polar bears, students may be asked to attend to the portion of the text that discusses the bears' habitat.

- A copy of the activity may be printed and displayed in the classroom or in students' individual literacy folders, providing students with a reference for retelling other expository texts.

- The activity may be used as part of an informal running record and included in documentation for comprehension of the text. After the students have completed the activity, print a copy and attach the running record.

- The number of *things I learned* may be adjusted according to students' abilities.

- Several activities may be used for a unit of study. The activities may then be printed and used as a study guide. Using symbols is recommended in this scenario. The symbols accompanied by text visually support the learning of the content.

Prior Knowledge: Personal Connections

Standards

✴ McREL Standards – Language Arts

(http://www.mcrel.org/standards-benchmarks/)

- Uses reading skills and strategies to understand and interpret a variety of literary texts

- Relates stories to personal experiences

✴ Grade Levels: K-2 (Ages 5-8)

Description

Comprehension is the ability to understand, remember and communicate ideas read. Active readers use comprehension strategies to make sense of text. Strategies include: inferring, making connections, determining importance, summarizing, questioning and synthesizing information. Active readers make connections between the text and their own lives. Readers are more engaged and comprehend better when they think about how the text relates to them, to other books they have read and to the world around them. Making connections on a personal level when reading text deepens the readers' understanding of the text, and thus supports comprehension. In this lesson, students will use a Kidspiration® activity to record their connections between the text and their own lives.

Instructions

1. Go to **Kidspiration 3 Teacher menu>Teacher Resources Online>Lesson Plans** and open the *Personal Connections.kia* activity, shown below, and review it with students.

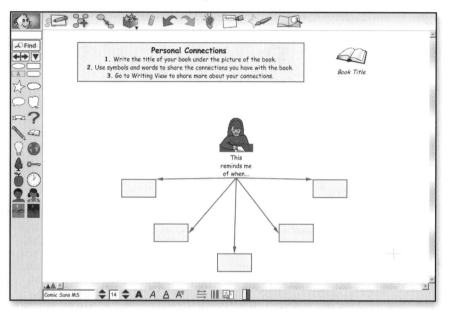

2. Explain that active readers make personal connections when they read. Situations and characters in the text remind readers of things that have happened in their own lives. This is often referred to as their *background knowledge*. Background knowledge helps readers understand the text.

3. Use a "think-aloud" to model for the students how readers connect personal experiences to text. Select a fictional text with a story that students are likely to relate to due to similar or shared experiences. A suggested text is *Julius, the Baby of the World* by Kevin Henkes or *The Relatives Came* by Cynthia Rylant. Both are stories about families. Stress that personal connections should deepen the readers understanding of the text. For example, saying, "Cinderella has a dress and so do I" does not help readers understand the text more deeply. Saying, "I have a pretty dress like Cinderella, and when I wear it I feel special" helps readers understand how Cinderella must have felt when she dressed for the ball.

   Note: If you would like to view an exemplar prior to modeling the lesson, review the *Connections Exemplar.kid* activity shown below.

Personal Connections
1. Write the title of your book under the picture of the book.
2. Use symbols and words to share the connections you have with the book.
3. Go to Writing View to share more about your connections.

Julius, The Baby of the World

This reminds me of when...

my little sister was born.

my mom snuggles and kisses me.

Jackie was not treating Tim nicely. I didn't like it either.

my family had the big party for my little sister.

my parents compliment me. It makes me feel good.

4. After you have modeled making personal connections, record the students' connections too, making sure the connections deepen the understanding of the text.

5. When students have had sufficient guided practice in completing the activity to record their personal connections, students should be allowed to complete an activity independently, reading text at their independent reading level.

Additional comprehension lessons can be located here: **Kidspiration 3 Teacher menu>Teacher Resources Online>Lesson Plans.**

Assessment

- Confirm the examples from the story relate to the experiences of the students and deepen the students' understanding of the text. Students should be able to explain how their experiences relate to those in the text.

Adaptations

- The same lesson format may be used to teach *text-to-text* and *text-to-world connections*. Students may also identify what type of connection they had with the book.

- Students can share orally or in **Writing View** how the connection deepened their understanding of the text.

- When completing the activity independently, students should read books at their independent reading level.

- The activity may also be used for expository texts. Students connect factual background knowledge to examples in the text rather than to personal experiences.

Storyboard

Standards

✴ McREL Standards – Language Arts

(http://www.mcrel.org/standards-benchmarks/)

- Uses reading skills and strategies to understand and interpret a variety of literary texts
- Knows the main ideas or theme of a story

✴ Grade Levels: K-2 (Ages 5-8)

Description

Comprehension is the ability to understand, remember and communicate ideas read. Active readers use comprehension strategies to make sense of text. Strategies include: inferring, making connections, determining importance, summarizing, questioning and synthesizing information. Whereas drawing is a thinking tool, this Kidspiration® activity provides a storyboarding framework from which students can summarize and retell a story.

Instructions

1. Go to **Kidspiration 3 Teacher menu>Teacher Resources Online>Lesson Plans** and open the *Storyboard.kia* activity, shown below, and review it with students.

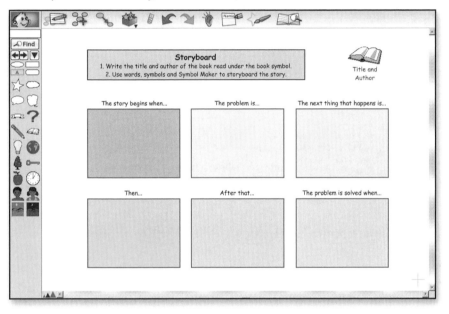

Explain that there are many ways for readers to share their knowledge of a story. When students retell, they share what was important, and retell the story in a way that makes sense. Students can talk or write about a story; today students will use pictures and a few words to retell a story.

2. Prior to reading a short fictional text selected for the lesson, remind students that the purpose of the reading is to be able to help them retell the story using the storyboard activity. A suggested story for this lesson is Robert Munsch's *Stephanie's Ponytail*. Its story structures are easily identifiable and the story is engaging.

3. Read the selected text.

4. Use a "think-aloud" to model completing the activity with information from the book.

   Note: If you would like to view an exemplar prior to modeling the lesson, review the *Storyboard Exemplar.kid* activity shown below, which was completed using the story *Stephanie's Ponytail*.

5. After modeling completing the activity, ask students to turn to a partner and take turns orally retelling the story following the storyboard.

6. After students have had sufficient guided practice in using the storyboard activity to retell stories, students should be allowed to complete an activity independently, reading text at their independent reading level.

Additional comprehension lessons can be located here: **Kidspiration 3 Teacher menu>Teacher Resources Online>Lesson Plans**.

Assessment

- Confirm that the storyboard retells the story read. Retelling should reveal an awareness of the text's content and contain accurate information.

Adaptations

- When completing the activity independently, students should read books at their independent reading level.

- Students may "read" their storyboards to a classmate when completed.

- The storyboard may be used as part of an informal running record and included in documentation for comprehension of the text. After the student has completed the storyboard, print a copy and attach the running record.

Inferring Word Meanings

Standards

⭐ McREL Standards – Language Arts

(http://www.mcrel.org/standards-benchmarks/)

- Uses the general skills and strategies of the reading process
- Uses meaning clues to aid comprehension and make predictions about content

⭐ Grade Levels: K-2 (Ages 5-8)

Description

Comprehension is the ability to understand, remember and communicate ideas read. Active readers use comprehension strategies to make sense of text. Strategies include: inferring, making connections, determining importance, summarizing, questioning and synthesizing information. A key to comprehending text is the ability to infer word meanings. This Kidspiration® activity provides a framework for students to use their background knowledge (schema), contextual clues and rereading to infer the meanings of words.

Instructions

1. Go to **Kidspiration 3 Teacher menu>Teacher Resources Online>Lesson Plans** and open the *Inferring Word Meanings.kia* activity, shown below, and review it with students.

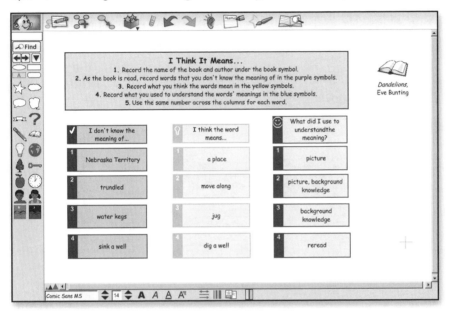

Explain that active readers infer many things when they read. Active readers read between the lines and use clues provided by the text, pictures and even their own background knowledge to infer. To demonstrate making an inference, pretend to order a pizza over the phone using words like: *medium, extra-cheese, thin crust* and *pepperoni*. Make sure to include an address while "placing your order" and ask, "How long will it be?" Do not use the word "pizza" in the role-playing. Ask students, "What have I just pretended to do?" They will answer, "Ordered pizza." Ask them how they knew given that you never used the word "pizza." Students will respond by giving examples of the words you did use. Explain to them that they just "read between the lines." They made an inference by using the clues you provided while role-playing ordering a pizza and their own knowledge of pizza. Explain that active readers make inferences about the meanings of new words while they read, just as they did when you pretended to order a pizza. Further explain that today they will look for clues in pictures and text and think about their own background knowledge to infer the meaning of new words. Readers need to learn to infer word meanings so they can understand what they read.

2. Select a short fictional text which contains words unknown to the students. Ensure that the word meanings can be inferred by using pictorial or contextual clues as well as students' background knowledge. A suggested text is *Where Are You Going, Manyoni?* by Catherine Stock.

3. Use a "think-aloud" to model completing the activity. Model and explain how various word meanings are inferred by using the illustrations, rereading, background knowledge, or a combination of the aforementioned.

   Note: If you would like to view an exemplar prior to modeling the lesson, review the *Word Meanings Exemplar.kid* shown below.

4. After students have had sufficient guided practice in inferring word meanings and determining how the word meaning was inferred, students should complete an activity independently, reading text at their independent reading level.

Additional comprehension lessons can be located here: **Kidspiration 3 Teacher menu>Teacher Resources Online>Lesson Plans.**

Assessment

- Confirm that the activity contains new vocabulary, plausible inferred meanings and reasonable explanations for how the word meaning was obtained.

Adaptations

- When completing the activity independently, students should read books at their independent reading level.

- Students can check their inferred word meaning using the Kidspiration **Word Guide.**

- The activity may be used with informational text in the same manner. The activity, once checked for accuracy, may be printed and used as a study guide.

- More than one activity can be used with a book.

Asking Questions

Standards

✦ McREL Standards – Language Arts

(http://www.mcrel.org/standards-benchmarks/)

- Uses reading skills and strategies to understand and interpret a variety of literary texts

✦ Grade Levels: K-2 (Ages 5-8)

Description

Comprehension is the ability to understand, remember and communicate ideas read. Active readers use comprehension strategies to make sense of text. Strategies include: inferring, making connections, determining importance, summarizing, questioning and synthesizing information. Active readers use many strategies as they read. When students ask questions, whether it be before, during or after they read, it engages them in the reading process. Questions help readers clarify and understand what they read. In this lesson, students use a Kidspiration® activity to support the use of asking questions and determining how the questions were answered.

Instructions

1. Prior to teaching the lesson, select a text which causes students to ask questions. Text suggestions are: *The Lotus Seed* by Sherry Garland, *Grandfather Twilight* by Barbara Berger, or Eve Bunting's *How Many Days to America?*

2. Go to **Kidspiration 3 Teacher menu>Teacher Resources Online>Lesson Plans and** open the *Asking Questions.kia* activity, shown below, and review it with students.

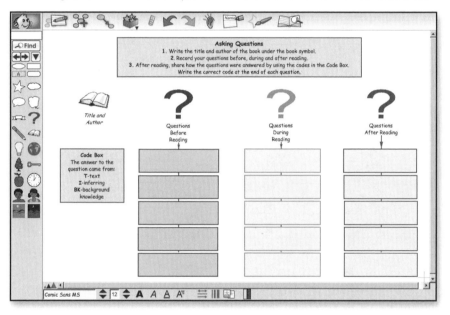

Explain that active readers ask questions before, during and after reading. Questioning helps readers set a purpose for their reading. After asking questions, readers read to find the answers. Today students will ask questions before, during and after reading, and then determine how the questions were answered. Were they answered in the text, by making an inference or because of the reader's background knowledge?

3. Use a "think-aloud" to model completing the activity.

   Note: If you would like to view an exemplar prior to teaching the lesson, open the *Asking Questions Exemplar.kid* activity shown below.

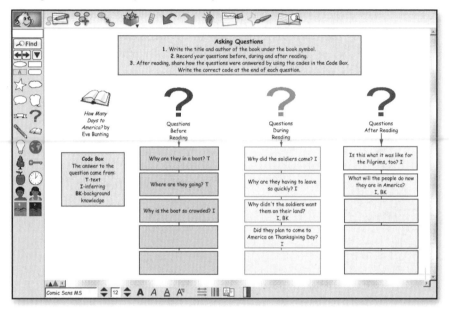

Again explain that active readers ask questions before, during and after reading. Model asking questions prior to reading the text by reading the pre-selected text's title and viewing the front cover. Record the questions.

4. Read the text and continue to record questions during reading.

5. After reading the text, record questions.

6. Explain to students that readers' questions can be answered in many ways. Answers may be inferred or answered by the readers' background knowledge, which may include information from other books or personal experiences. An answer may also be stated in the text. Sometimes questions can be answered by using a combination, for example from background knowledge and by making an inference.

7. Using the codes from the *Code Box*, model deciding how a question was answered and code the question appropriately. Finish coding the remainder of the questions.

8. When students have had sufficient guided practice in completing the activity, have students complete an activity independently, reading text at their independent reading level. Remind students that active readers ask questions before, during and after reading to help them set a purpose for reading. Active readers also think about how their questions were answered.

Additional comprehension lessons can be located here: **Kidspiration 3 Teacher menu> Teacher Resources Online>Lesson Plans**.

Assessment

- Questions should relate to the content of the text.
- Confirm that the questions are coded correctly.

Adaptations

- When completing the activity independently, students should read books at their independent reading level.
- More than one activity may be used for a text.
- Students may switch to **Writing View** and explain in writing how the question was answered, providing specific details.
- The activity may be utilized with fictional or expository text.

Synthesizing Text: The Big Idea

Standards

✦ McREL Standards – Language Arts

(http://www.mcrel.org/standards-benchmarks/)

- Uses reading skills and strategies to understand and interpret a variety of literary texts
- Knows the main ideas or theme of a story

✦ Grade Levels: K-2 (Ages 5-8)

Description

Comprehension is the ability to understand, remember and communicate ideas read. Active readers use comprehension strategies to make sense of text. Strategies include: inferring, making connections, determining importance, summarizing, questioning and synthesizing information. Young readers synthesize text when they retell a story. Young readers also synthesize text when they identify the big idea or theme of a story. This Kidspiration® lesson provides a framework from which students can synthesize the text, identifying the theme of a story while showing how their thinking evolved.

Instructions

1. Select a text for the lesson which allows the reader's thinking to evolve and contains a theme. Suggested texts are: *An Angel for Solomon* by Cynthia Rylant, *The Rag Coat* by Lauren Mills, *Smoky Night* by Eve Bunting or John Steptoe's *The Story of Jumping Mouse*. Fables may also be used.

2. Go to **Kidspiration 3 Teacher menu>Teacher Resources Online>Lesson Plans** and open the *The Big Idea.kia* activity, shown below, and review it with students.

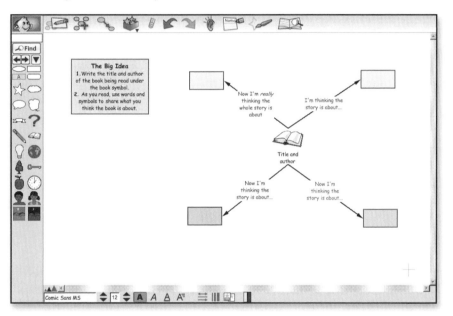

Share with students that they will be using the activity to record their thinking about what is the book's big idea or theme. Explain that the big idea or theme is the big message or the most important idea the author wants the reader to remember. As active readers, our ideas of what a book is about change as we read. It starts small and grows. Use the analogy of throwing a rock into a pond. First there's a splash, and then ripples appear, getting larger as they spread out. When we do that, it's called *synthesizing*. Our ideas grow just like the ripples in the pond.

Note: Use and define the term *synthesizing* for students at your own discretion.

3. Use a "think-aloud" to model completing the activity, reading the pre-selected text.

   Note: If you would like to view an exemplar prior to modeling the lesson, review the *Big Idea Exemplar.kid* activity shown below.

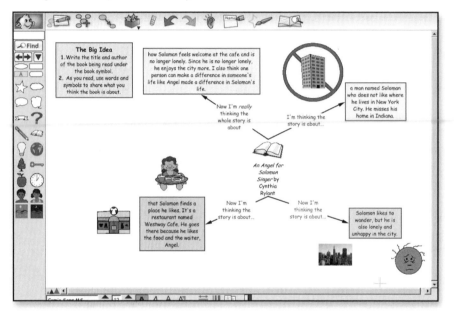

4. After students have had sufficient guided practice in completing the activity, students should complete the activity independently, reading text at their independent reading level. Prior to students beginning, remind them that the big idea or theme is the big message or the most important idea the author wants the reader to remember. As active readers read, their ideas of what a book is about change. It starts small and grows. The ideas grow bigger as we read. (Remind students of the rock and pond analogy.) When our thinking grows like the ripples in the pond, it's called *synthesizing*. Synthesizing helps us understand and remember what we read.

Additional comprehension lessons can be located here: **Kidspiration 3 Teacher menu>Teacher Resources Online>Lesson Plans.**

Assessment

- Confirm that students complete the activity using evolving thoughts.

Adaptations

- When completing the activity independently, students should read books at their independent reading level.

- If several students read the same story, have them discuss the theme. Assist students in discovering that a story may have more than one theme, and the same theme can be stated in several ways.

Creating Mental Images

Standards

✦ McREL Standards – Language Arts

(http://www.mcrel.org/standards-benchmarks/)

- Uses reading skills and strategies to understand and interpret a variety of literary texts
- Uses mental images based on pictures and print to aid in comprehension of text

✦ Grade Levels: K-2 (Ages 5-8)

Description

Comprehension is the ability to understand, remember and communicate ideas read. Active readers use comprehension strategies to make sense of text. Strategies include: inferring, making connections, determining importance, summarizing, questioning and synthesizing information. Active readers use many strategies as they read. When a reader visualizes a scene from a book, the mental images are created because the reader is also inferring. Visualizing and inferring occur simultaneously. When readers visualize, they create pictures unique to them in their minds. This Kidspiration® activity provides a framework for students to share their visual pictures.

Instructions

1. Prior to teaching the lesson, select a text which creates strong visual images. A portion of a text may be used rather than an entire text. A suggested text is E.B. White's *Charlotte's Web*, Chapter 3, the pages which contain the description of the barn.

2. Go to **Kidspiration 3 Teacher menu>Teacher Resources Online>Lesson Plans** and open the *Creating Mental Images.kia* activity, shown below, and review it with students.

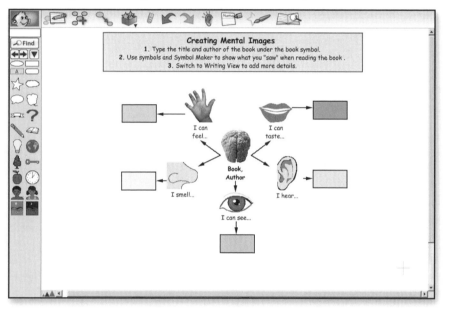

Explain that active readers create pictures in their minds while reading. They create a "movie" in their head of what is being read. Those pictures are unique to the reader and no two readers visualize or "see" the same thing.

Note: A teacher may wish to read a book and then view a movie of the same story. Discuss the differences between what the readers visualized versus what was depicted in the movie.

3. Prior to reading the text selected for the lesson, remind students that as they read they should be aware of the pictures they are creating from the text as they will be helping you complete the activity.

Note: If you would like to view an exemplar prior to modeling the lesson, review the *Mental Images Exemplar.kid* activity shown below.

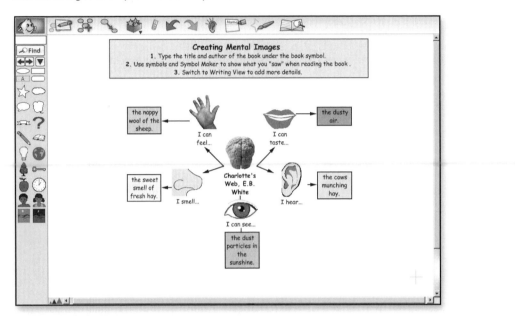

4. Read the text.

5. Use a "think-aloud" to model completing the activity. Discuss how different readers' images were different, no two being alike.

   Note: The teacher may wish to explain that when a reader visualizes a scene from a book, the mental images are created because the reader is also *inferring*. *Visualizing* and *inferring* occur simultaneously.

6. After students have had sufficient guided practice in completing the activity, students can complete an activity independently, reading text at their independent reading level.

   Note: Depending on the students' reading level, the text may include illustrations. Explain to students that even with illustrations in books, we still create our own pictures from the words and illustrations. Remind students that active readers use many strategies while reading, and visualizing helps them "see" and understand the story.

Additional comprehension lessons can be located here: **Kidspiration 3 Teacher menu>Teacher Resources Online>Lesson Plans.**

Assessment

- Confirm that students completed the activity using symbols and words that represent ideas and concepts from the text.

Adaptations

- For text that contains chapters, an activity may be used for each chapter.

- The activity may be used for informational text as well.

- When completing the activity independently, students should read text at their independent reading level.

Definition by Association

Standards

✦ McREL Standards – Language Arts

(http://www.mcrel.org/standards-benchmarks/)

- Uses the general skills and strategies of the reading process
- Uses word reference materials to determine the meaning, pronunciation and derivations of unknown words

✦ Grade Levels: 3-5 (Ages 8-11)

Description

Vocabulary knowledge is the ability to remember and utilize word meanings and pronunciations. Students learn vocabulary through wide-reading as well as direct instruction. In addition to helping students improve comprehension and organize ideas for writing, Kidspiration® can be used as a tool to help students learn and apply vocabulary skills, supporting the teacher's reading curriculum.

Related to vocabulary instruction there are two principles essentially agreed upon: the relationship between vocabulary and reading comprehension is significant, and poor vocabulary is detrimental to the academic success of students. For disadvantaged students especially, vocabulary deficiency is primary in accounting for academic failure. The more words a student understands, the easier it is to understand what is read. The more terms a student knows related to a given topic, the easier it is to read, understand and learn additional information about the topic. Though no single approach to vocabulary instruction is most effective, active student engagement is key. This Kidspiration activity encourages students to become active learners as they make connections between words, concepts and visual representations, thus providing visual and textual support when learning new vocabulary.

Instructions

1. Discuss with students how important it is as readers to learn and remember new vocabulary. Understanding new vocabulary helps us understand and remember what we read. Go to **Kidspiration 3 Teacher menu>Teacher Resources Online>Lesson Plans** and open the *Definition by Association.kia* activity, shown below, and review it with students.

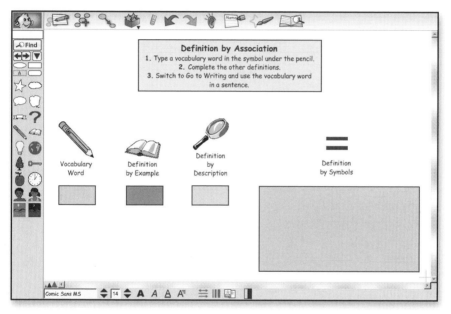

Explain to students that as learners we more easily remember new words when we can link them to our background knowledge, i.e., to what we already know. Further explain that a visual representation of a word is easily remembered and can help us remember what a word means. Share that they will use the *Definition by Association* activity to learn and remember new vocabulary associated with units of study.

2. Using a word from a current unit of study, model completing the activity using a "think-aloud."

Note: If you would like to view an exemplar prior to teaching the lesson, open the *Association Exemplar.kid* activity shown below.

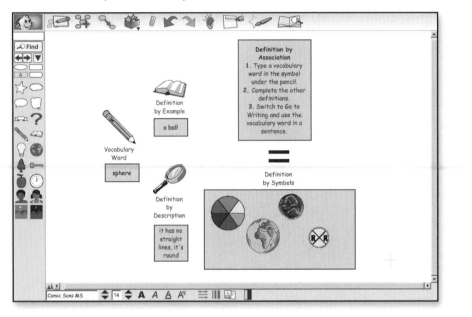

3. Remind students that understanding new vocabulary helps the reader understand and remember the author's message. After students have had sufficient guided practice in completing the activity, assign students vocabulary words and have them complete the activity independently, using one activity per word.

Additional vocabulary lessons can be located here: **Kidspiration 3 Teacher menu>Teacher Resources Online>Lesson Plans.**

Assessment

- Confirm that students have completed the activity, and the text and visual representations of the vocabulary words are appropriate and accurate.

Adaptations

- Several activities can be utilized for a unit of study.

- Activities can be printed and used as a study guide.

- Students can switch to **Writing View** and add additional information about the vocabulary word or notes from class.

- Depending on the content and purpose of the vocabulary study, students may self-select words to add to the activity.

Theme or Topic Web

Standards

✦ McREL Standards – Language Arts

(http://www.mcrel.org/standards-benchmarks/)

- Uses the general skills and strategies of the reading process
- Understands level-appropriate reading vocabulary

✦ Grade Levels: 3-5 (Ages 8-11)

Description

Vocabulary knowledge is the ability to remember and utilize word meanings and pronunciations. Students learn vocabulary through wide-reading as well as direct instruction. In addition to helping students improve comprehension and organize ideas for writing, Kidspiration® can be used as a tool to help students learn and apply vocabulary skills, supporting the teacher's reading curriculum.

Related to vocabulary instruction there are two principles essentially agreed upon: the relationship between vocabulary and reading comprehension is significant, and poor vocabulary is detrimental to the academic success of students. For disadvantaged students especially, vocabulary deficiency is primary in accounting for academic failure. The more words a student understands, the easier it is to understand what is read. The more terms a student knows related to a given topic, the easier it is to read, understand and learn additional information about the topic. Though no single approach to vocabulary instruction is most effective, active student engagement is key. This Kidspiration activity encourages students to develop vocabulary associated with a theme or topic, extending their thinking over a period of time.

Instructions

1. This activity is meant to be used when beginning a new unit of study and over a period of several days.

2. Go to **Kidspiration 3 Teacher menu>Teacher Resources Online>Lesson Plans** and open the *Theme or Topic Web.kia* activity, shown below, and review it with students.

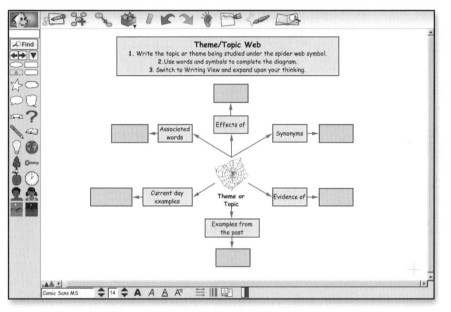

Explain to students that they will use this activity as they begin a new unit of study. Using this activity, students will first share what they know about a topic currently, and then extend their ideas and vocabulary as they learn more.

Note: If you would like to see an exemplar prior to teaching the lesson, open the *Theme or Topic Exemplar.kid* activity shown below.

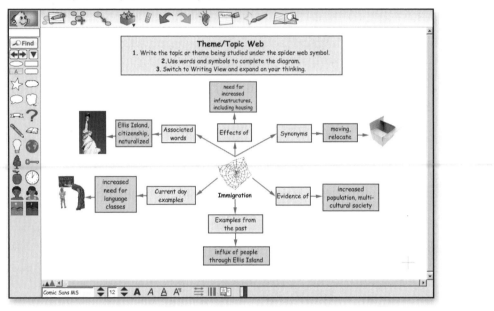

3. Using a topic or theme from the unit of study, ask students to complete the activity. This initial completed activity will provide the teacher with information related to students' current knowledge of the topic including topic vocabulary. After students have completed the initial activity, have students switch to **Writing View** and print a copy. Assess the activities for the students' current knowledge, including topic misunderstandings, and plan accordingly.

4. During and at the end of the unit of study, have students use the activity to record their academic understanding of the topic or theme. The *Theme or Topic Web.kia* activity will support students learning the attributes of the topic or theme.

5. After the final activity has been completed, have students switch to **Writing View** and print a copy of the activity.

Additional vocabulary lessons can be located here: **Kidspiration 3 Teacher menu>Teacher Resources Online>Lesson Plans**.

Assessment

- Confirm that students have completed the activity with examples appropriate to the theme or topic.

- Compare the initial activity with the students' final activity. Evaluate the increased level of understanding and use of vocabulary between the two activities.

Adaptations

- Several activities can be utilized for a unit of study. Use one activity for each major theme or topic in the unit. Depending on the content and purpose of the unit of study, students may self-select the theme or topic.

Contextual Definitions

Standards

✦ McREL Standards – Language Arts

(http://www.mcrel.org/standards-benchmarks/)

- Uses the general skills and strategies of the reading process
- Understands level-appropriate reading vocabulary
- Uses a variety of context clues to decode unknown words

✦ Grade Levels: 3-5 (Ages 8-11)

Description

Vocabulary knowledge is the ability to remember and utilize word meanings and pronunciations. Students learn vocabulary through wide-reading as well as direct instruction. In addition to helping students improve comprehension and organize ideas for writing, Kidspiration® can be used as a tool to help students learn and apply vocabulary skills, supporting the teacher's reading curriculum.

Related to vocabulary instruction there are two principles essentially agreed upon: the relationship between vocabulary and reading comprehension is significant, and poor vocabulary is detrimental to the academic success of students. For disadvantaged students especially, vocabulary deficiency is primary in accounting for academic failure. The more words a student understands, the easier it is to understand what is read. The more terms a student knows related to a given topic, the easier it is to read, understand and learn additional information about the topic. Though no single approach to vocabulary instruction is most effective, active student engagement is key. As mentioned previously, students acquire a great deal of vocabulary from wide-reading, using contextual clues to determine the meanings of unknown words. This Kidspiration activity encourages students to become active learners as they infer word meanings from contextual clues.

Instructions

1. Prior to the lesson, select a text or a portion of a text that contains words that will be unknown to the majority of the students, and also contains contextual support to allow for the words' meanings to be inferred.

2. Discuss with students how important it is as readers to learn and remember new vocabulary. Understanding new vocabulary helps us not only understand and remember what we read, but makes it easier for us to learn new information. Explain that active readers can infer word meaning by using the contextual clues from the sentences before and after the unknown word and how the word is *used* in the sentence (syntax).
Go to **Kidspiration 3 Teacher menu>Teacher Resources Online>Lesson Plans** and open the *Contextual Definitions.kia* activity, shown below, and review it with students.

3. Using a "think-aloud," model completing the activity. When modeling, show students how you infer a word's meaning, pointing out the clues from the text which support inferring the word's meaning. When appropriate, point out sentence syntax and its use in determining word meaning as well.

Note: If you would like to view an exemplar prior to teaching the lesson, open the *Definitions Exemplar.kid* activity shown below.

I Think It Means...

1. Record the name of the book and author under the book symbol.
2. As the book is read, record words that you don't know the meaning of in the purple symbols.
3. Record what you think the words mean in the yellow symbols.
4. Record what you used to understand the words' meanings in the blue symbols.
5. Use the same number across the columns for each word.

Dandelions, Eve Bunting

I don't know the meaning of...	I think the word means...	What did I use to understand the meaning?
1 Nebraska Territory	1 a place	1 picture
2 trundled	2 move along	2 picture, background knowledge
3 water kegs	3 jug	3 background knowledge
4 sink a well	4 dig a well	4 reread

Comic Sans MS   14

4. After the students have had sufficient guided practice inferring word meanings from contextual clues, have students complete the activity independently, reading at their independent reading level. Remind students that active readers learn the meaning of many words by using contextual clues when reading.

Additional vocabulary lessons can be located here: **Kidspiration 3 Teacher menu>Teacher Resources Online>Lesson Plans.**

Assessment

- Confirm that students have completed the activity making inferences based on the contextual clues provided.

Adaptations

- The lesson can be used with fictional as well as expository text.

- Have students switch to **Writing View** and use the Kidspiration **Word Guide** or another reference material to confirm or adjust their definitions.

- When completing the activity independently, students should read text at their independent reading level.

Alphabet Cards

Standards

✦ McREL Standards – Language Arts

(http://www.mcrel.org/standards-benchmarks/)

- Uses the general skills and strategies of the reading process
- Understands level-appropriate reading vocabulary

✦ Grade Levels: 3-5 (Ages 8-11)

Description

Vocabulary knowledge is the ability to remember and utilize word meanings and pronunciations. Students learn vocabulary through wide-reading as well as direct instruction. In addition to helping students improve comprehension and organize ideas for writing, Kidspiration® can be used as a tool to help students learn and apply vocabulary skills, supporting the teacher's reading curriculum.

Related to vocabulary instruction there are two principles essentially agreed upon: the relationship between vocabulary and reading comprehension is significant, and poor vocabulary is detrimental to the academic success of students. For disadvantaged students especially, vocabulary deficiency is primary in accounting for academic failure. The more words a student understands, the easier it is for them to understand what they read. The more terms a student knows related to a given topic, the easier it is for them to read, understand and learn additional information about the topic. Though no single approach to vocabulary instruction is most effective, active student engagement is key. Building and expanding vocabulary are key to comprehension in the content areas. This Kidspiration lesson engages students and helps deepen their understanding of vocabulary and content in a creative and fun manner. Students select pictorial representations for each letter of the alphabet that will help them remember and understand content vocabulary and concepts.

Instructions

1. Collect several high-level alphabet books to have in the classroom. A few suggested titles include: *Arctic Alphabet*: *Exploring the North from A to Z* by W. Lynch; *V for Vanishing: an Alphabet of Endangered Animals* by P. Mullins; *Ashanti to Zulu: African Traditions* by M. Musgrove; *A is for Appalachia: the Alphabet Book of Appalachian Heritage* by L.H. Pack; and *A Walk in the Rainforest* by K. Pratt. For other suggested titles, speak to an elementary school or public librarian.

2. Read one or two of the sample alphabet books aloud to the students. Discuss the structures and purpose of each text. Note that alphabet books written for young children teach students the letters of the alphabet, whereas alphabet books written for older students teach content.

3. Go to **Kidspiration 3 Teacher menu>Teacher Resources Online>Lesson Plans** and open the *Alphabet Cards Exemplar.kid* activity, shown below, and review it with students.

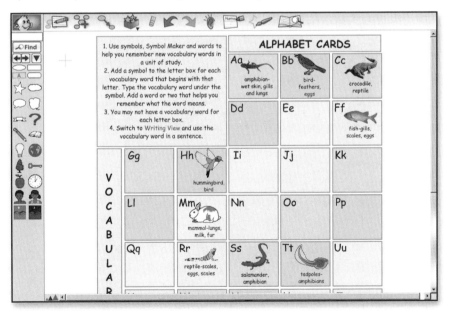

Explain to students that they will write mini-versions of alphabet books during a unit of study. Explain that the pictorial representation for a word should be a symbol that helps them define and remember the word or concept. Students may use the Kidspiration **Word Guide** as a resource to define words and look for synonyms.

4. A list of specific vocabulary words to be used in the activity may be provided for the students. When students understand the activity directions, go to **Kidspiration 3 Teacher menu>Teacher Resources Online>Lesson Plans** and open the *Alphabet Card.kia* activity shown below. Instruct the students to complete the activity independently.

ALPHABET CARDS

1. Use symbols, Symbol Maker and words to help you remember new vocabulary words in a unit of study.
2. Add a symbol to the letter box for each vocabulary word that begins with that letter. Type the vocabulary word under the symbol. Add a word or two that helps you remember what the word means.
3. You may not have a vocabulary word for each letter box.
4. Switch to Writing View and use the vocabulary word in a sentence.

| | Aa | Bb | Cc |
| | Dd | Ee | Ff |

VOCABULARY

Gg	Hh	Ii	Jj	Kk
Ll	Mm	Nn	Oo	Pp
Qq	Rr	Ss	Tt	Uu
Vv	Ww	Xx	Yy	Zz

✓ Assessment

- Confirm that students' definitions and explanations are correct.

Adaptations

- In addition to providing students with a list of words that should be included in the activity, a given number of hyperlinks may be required within the activity.

- Students may work in small groups to complete the activity.

- Students may submit a list of vocabulary words to the teacher for approval prior to completing the activity.

- Since units can be lengthy, the activity may be completed for a specific portion of the unit.

- The students' activities may be printed in **Writing View** and/or in **Picture View** to be utilized as study guides.

Affix Web

Standards

✴ McREL Standards – Language Arts

(http://www.mcrel.org/standards-benchmarks/)

- Uses the general skills and strategies of the reading process
- Understands level-appropriate reading vocabulary
- Uses word reference materials to determine the meaning, pronunciation and derivations of unknown words
- Uses phonetic and structural analysis techniques, syntactic structure and semantic context to decode unknown words

✴ Grade Levels: 3-5 (Ages 8-11)

Description

Vocabulary knowledge is the ability to remember and utilize word meanings and pronunciations. Students learn vocabulary through wide-reading as well as direct instruction. In addition to helping students improve comprehension and organize ideas for writing, Kidspiration® can be used as a tool to help students learn and apply vocabulary skills, supporting the teacher's reading curriculum.

Related to vocabulary instruction there are two principles essentially agreed upon: the relationship between vocabulary and reading comprehension is significant, and poor vocabulary is detrimental to the academic success of students. For disadvantaged students especially, vocabulary deficiency is primary in accounting for academic failure. The more words a student understands, the easier it is to understand what is read. The more terms a student knows related to a given topic, the easier it is to read, understand and learn additional information about the topic. Though no single approach to vocabulary instruction is most effective, active student engagement is key. Students who know the meaning of affixes have a valuable tool when attempting to understand the meaning of new words. This activity encourages students to become active learners as they learn the meaning of affixes using the Kidspiration **Word Guide**, by associating words and visual representations to affixes.

Instructions

1. Discuss with students how important it is as readers to learn and remember new vocabulary. Understanding new vocabulary helps us to not only understand and remember what we read, but makes it easier for us to learn new information. Go to **Kidspiration 3 Teacher menu>Teacher Resources Online>Lesson Plans** and open the *Affix Web.kia* activity, shown below, and review it with students.

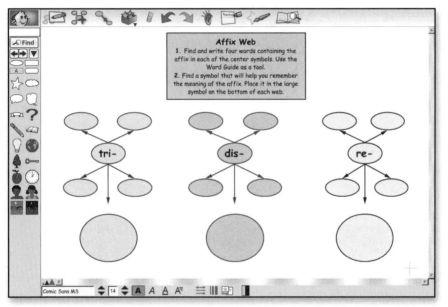

2. Explain to students that many words we read contain affixes (prefixes or suffixes). Further explain that if readers know the meaning of the affix, they can often determine the meaning of an unknown word. Share that they will use the *Affix Web.kia* activity to learn and remember the meaning of affixes.

3. Model completing the activity.

   Note: If you would like to view an exemplar prior to teaching the lesson, open the *Affix Web Exemplar.kid* activity shown below.

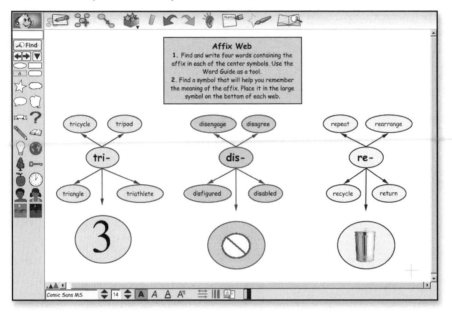

4. Remind students that as readers it's important to understand and remember the meaning of new words. Understanding the meaning of affixes helps readers understand the meaning of many unknown words. Have students complete the activity independently.

Additional vocabulary lessons can be located here: **Kidspiration 3 Teacher menu>Teacher Resources Online>Lesson Plans.**

Assessment

- Confirm that students have completed the activity using words containing the correct affixes and that the symbol association is accurate.

Adaptations

- The affixes within the activity can be changed to meet the needs of the students and teacher.

- Activities can be printed and used as a study guide.

What's It Matter?

Standards

✴ McREL Standards – Language Arts

(http://www.mcrel.org/standards-benchmarks/)

- Uses reading skills and strategies to understand and interpret a variety of informational texts
- Summarizes and paraphrases information in texts

✴ Grade Levels: 3-5 (Ages 8-11)

Description

Comprehension is the ability to understand, remember and communicate ideas read. Active readers use comprehension strategies to make sense of text. Strategies include: inferring, making connections, determining importance, summarizing, questioning and synthesizing information. As active readers, we remember what we find to be relevant and important; we remember what matters. When reading expository text, readers need to construct meaning from the new information, and find the new information's importance and relevancy to their lives and the world around them. This Kidspiration® activity supports readers in learning new content and making the learning relevant to their own lives.

Instructions

1. Go to **Kidspiration 3 Teacher menu>Teacher Resources Online>Lesson Plans** and open the *What's It Matter Exemplar.kid* activity, shown below, and review it with students. Explain that active readers construct meaning as they learn new content. They construct meaning by determining how the information is relevant or important, how it connects to them, their families and the world around them. They determine why the information matters. The exemplar below shows one reader's thinking, recorded on the activity while learning new information or content.

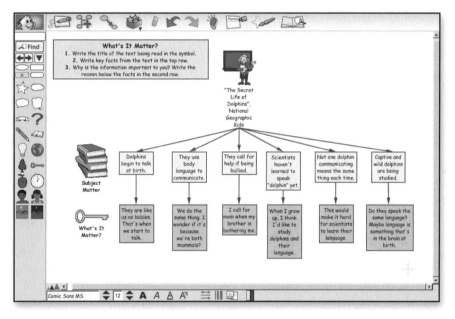

2. Now open the *What's It Matter.kia* activity, shown below, and review it with students. Using a short informational text selected for the lesson, model completing the activity using a "think-aloud." High-interest text from magazines or trade books, appropriate to grade-level, work well. Depending on the age of the students, articles from a local or school newspaper work well also. Record paraphrased information from the text in the symbols in the first row. Determine if students should record paraphrased information in note form or complete sentences, and model accordingly.

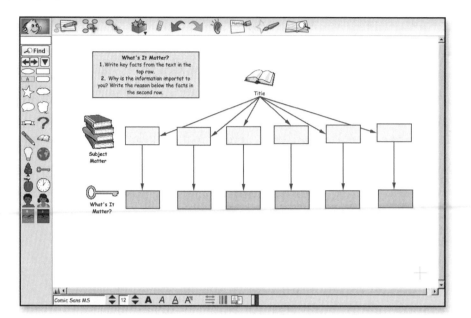

3. After recording information from the text, record why the information is relevant or important in the *What's It Matter?* row. Symbols from the **Symbol palette** may replace the rectangle symbols in the activity to communicate ideas. Replace the rectangle symbols with a newly selected symbol and add text. Explain to students that this portion of the activity is where they construct meaning by determining how the information is relevant or important, i.e., how it connects to them, their families and the world around them. It is where they determine and write why the information matters to them individually. Again, decide if information should be written in note form or complete sentences.

4. After students have had sufficient guided practice in completing the activity, have students complete the activity independently, reading text at their independent reading level. Prior to independent use, remind students that active readers remember what they find to be relevant and important; they remember what matters. When reading expository text, readers need to construct meaning from the new information, and find the new information's importance and relevancy to their lives and the world around them.

Additional comprehension lessons can be located here: **Kidspiration 3 Teacher menu>Teacher Resources Online>Lesson Plans.**

✓ Assessment

- Students should have recorded important information from the text.

- Confirm that what the students have recorded in *What's It Matter?* indicates use of background knowledge and the new content. Responses should indicate a higher level of cognitive processing and real-world applications.

Adaptations

- Several activities may be used in a unit of study or for use with longer text.

- The Kidspiration **Word Guide** can be helpful to students, to clarify word meaning when reading text.

- Have students share their responses to *What's It Matter?*, providing additional opportunities for content discussion as well as varying perspectives.

- When completing the activity independently, students should read text at their independent reading level.

Reflecting on Text

Standards

✴ McREL Standards – Language Arts

(http://www.mcrel.org/standards-benchmarks/)

- Uses reading skills and strategies to understand and interpret a variety of informational texts
- Monitors own reading strategies and makes modifications as needed
- Summarizes and paraphrases information in texts

✴ Grade Levels: 3-5 (Ages 8-11)

Description

Comprehension is the ability to understand, remember and communicate ideas read. Active readers use comprehension strategies to make sense of text. Strategies include: inferring, making connections, determining importance, summarizing, questioning and synthesizing information. Active readers reflect on what they read. This includes thinking about what they learned, what they found to be particularly interesting and asking questions after the text is read. This Kidspiration® activity supports readers as they reflect on informational text read.

Instructions

1. Go to **Kidspiration 3 Teacher menu>Teacher Resources Online>Lesson Plans** and open the *Reflecting On Text.kia* activity, shown below, and review it with students. Explain that active readers reflect on what they read by continuing to think about the text after the reading is completed. They summarize what they learned, think about what was especially interesting to them and ask questions after the reading is completed. When formulating questions, readers apply what they already know about a topic combined with the new information from the text.

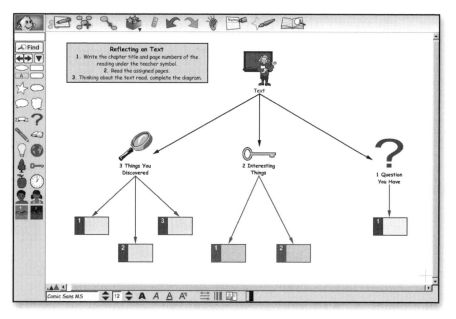

2. Use a "think-aloud" to model how to complete the activity using pages from a science or social studies textbook or another short expository text.

Note: If you would like to view an exemplar prior to teaching the lesson, open the *Reflecting On Text Exemplar.kid* activity shown below.

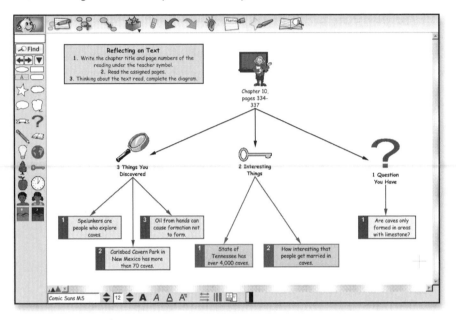

3. After students have had sufficient guided practice in completing the activity, have students complete the activity independently, reading text at their independent reading level. Remind students prior to use that active readers reflect on what they read by continuing to think about the text after the reading is completed. They summarize what was learned, consider what was interesting and ask questions when the reading is complete. Those questions are formulated based on background knowledge and the new information from the text.

Additional comprehension lessons can be located here: **Kidspiration 3 Teacher menu>Teacher Resources Online>Lesson Plans**.

✓ Assessment

- Students should have completed the activity with information from the text.

- Confirm that the students' questions are relevant to the topic and based on prior knowledge and new information.

Adaptations

- Several activities may be used in a unit of study.

- When completing the activity independently, students should read text at their independent reading level.

- The diagram may be used with fictional text as well.

Preview, Predict and Confirm

Standards

✦ McREL Standards – Language Arts

(http://www.mcrel.org/standards-benchmarks/)

- Uses reading skills and strategies to understand and interpret a variety of informational texts
- Summarizes and paraphrases information in texts
- Previews text
- Establishes a purpose for reading

✦ Grade Levels: 3-5 (Ages 8-11)

Description

Comprehension is the ability to understand, remember and communicate ideas read. Active readers use comprehension strategies to make sense of text. Strategies include: inferring, making connections, determining importance, summarizing, questioning and synthesizing information. Active readers use many strategies as they read. Prior to reading, they predict the vocabulary and content of the text, and activate prior knowledge. During reading, active readers ask questions, establishing a purpose for reading. After reading, active readers confirm whether their questions were answered and summarize what they have learned. These reading skills and strategies help readers understand a variety of text. In this lesson, students use a Kidspiration® activity to preview, predict, question and confirm their learning in informational text.

Instructions

1. Explain that active readers use many strategies before, during and after reading informational text. Today they will learn how to apply several of those strategies. Explain that active readers preview informational text to see what they will read about. Additionally, reading the questions at the end of the chapter helps readers predict and attend to the key points in the text. Active readers also ask their own questions as they read, and confirm and summarize what they learned after reading. These strategies help readers remember what they have read.

2. Go to **Kidspiration 3 Teacher menu>Teacher Resources Online>Lesson Plans** and open the *Preview, Predict, Confirm.kia* activity, shown below, and review it with students. Explain that this activity will support them in being active readers.

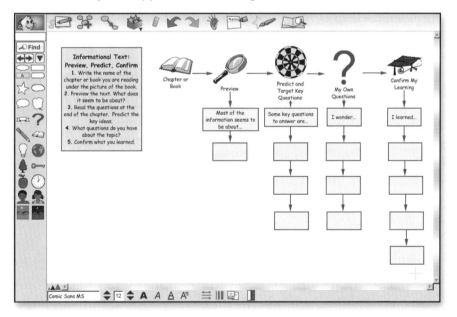

3. Use a "think-aloud" to model how to complete the activity using a chapter from a science or social studies textbook.

   Note: If you would like to view an exemplar prior to teaching the lesson, open the *Preview, Predict, Exemplar.kid* activity shown below.

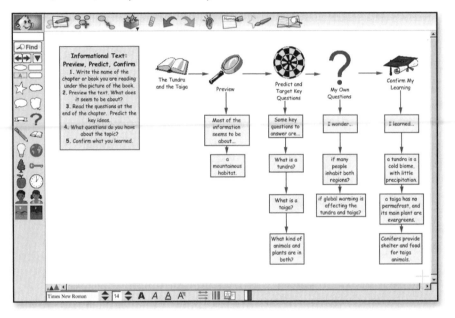

4. Preview the chapter title, headings, subtitles, photos, etc. Record what the chapter seems to be about under the *Preview* symbol.

5. Discuss how reading the end of chapter questions helps set a purpose for reading and helps readers attend to the key ideas in the material. This is especially important in high interest texts which include many interesting details about the topic. After reading the end of chapter questions, rephrase the questions and record them under the *Predict and Target Key Questions* symbol.

6. Explain that active readers ask their own questions while reading. Record individual questions under the *My Own Questions* symbol.

7. Summarize what you learned from reading the text. This should include the answers to the questions asked under the *Predict and Target Key Questions* symbol. Explain that questions asked in the *My Own Questions* may not always be answered in the text.

8. Once students have had sufficient guided practice using the activity, have students complete the activity independently, reading text at their independent reading level. Prior to use, remind students that active readers use many strategies as they read.

Additional comprehension lessons can be located here: **Kidspiration 3 Teacher menu>Teacher Resources Online>Lesson Plans.**

Assessment

- Students should have completed the activity with information from the text.

- The *Predict and Target Key Questions* should reflect the end of chapter questions.

- The students' questions should be relevant to the topic.

- The key points should be included in the *Confirm My Learning* portion of the activity.

Adaptations

- Several activities may be used in a unit of study. The activities may be printed and used as a study guide.

- If using a text that does not contain end of chapter questions, the classroom teacher may provide questions to help readers predict and focus on the key points within the text.

- Switch to **Writing View** and use the information as an outline for a report. This view may also be used as a study guide.

- When completing the activity independently, students should read text at their independent reading level.

Generating Questions

Standards

✳ McREL Standards – Language Arts

(http://www.mcrel.org/standards-benchmarks/)

- Uses reading skills and strategies to understand and interpret a variety of informational texts
- Summarizes and paraphrases information in texts
- Uses prior knowledge and experience to understand and respond to new information

✳ Grade Levels: 3-5 (Ages 8-11)

Description

Comprehension is the ability to understand, remember and communicate ideas read. Active readers use comprehension strategies to make sense of text. Strategies include: inferring, making connections, determining importance, summarizing, questioning and synthesizing information. Active readers use many strategies as they read. When students ask questions, whether it be before, during or after they read, it engages them in the reading process. Questions help readers clarify and understand what they read. In this Kidspiration® lesson, students use text features to preview text, record their questions to establish a purpose for reading and record the answers as they read.

Instructions

1. Explain that active readers use many strategies before, during and after reading informational text, one of them being asking questions. Go to **Kidspiration 3 Teacher menu>Teacher Resources Online>Lesson Plans and** open the *Generating Questions.kia* activity, shown below, and review it with students.

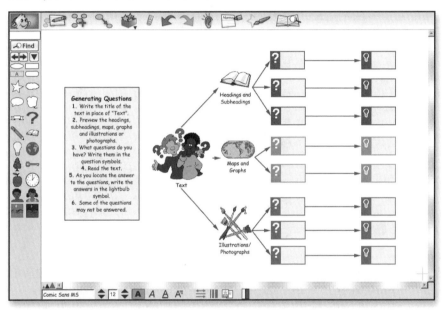

Also share that readers often ignore the text features found in informational text. Text features include headings, subheadings, maps, photos, options, etc. Text features are a significant source of information and can help readers ask questions, setting a purpose for reading.

Explain that questioning helps readers set a purpose for reading. Questioning helps them focus and think about what they will learn and what they want to learn. After asking questions, readers read to find the answers. Today they will preview the headings, subheadings, maps, graphs, and illustrations or photographs and generate questions, recording their answers as they read.

2. Using a chapter or lesson from a content area text book, complete the activity. Model asking questions after reviewing the texts' headings and subheadings, maps and graphs, illustrations or photographs, and captions.

Note: If you would like to view an exemplar prior to teaching the lesson, open the *Questions.kid* activity shown below.

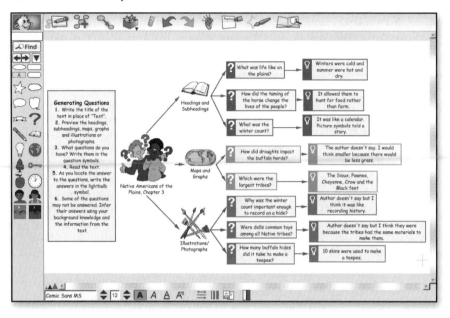

3. Record the questions in the corresponding symbols labeled with a question mark. Stress that when an answer to a question has been located, the information recorded in the activity is summarized and paraphrased in the students' own words, not copied directly from the text. The answers to questions are recorded in the corresponding symbols labeled with a lightbulb.

4. Explain that in some cases, questions asked by readers may not be answered by the author. Rather than ignoring those questions, active readers use information from the text and their background knowledge to draw a logical conclusion or infer an answer to the question. For an example, open the *Questions Exemplar.kid* activity and note the first question in *Maps and Graphs*. Model such a scenario. Explain your thinking, citing information from the text and sharing your background knowledge that supported the conclusion.

5. After students have had sufficient guided practice using the activity, have students complete the activity independently, reading text at their independent reading level. Prior to use, remind students that informational text features are a significant source of information and can help readers ask questions, setting a purpose for reading.

Additional comprehension lessons can be located here: **Kidspiration 3 Teacher menu>Teacher Resources Online>Lesson Plans.**

Assessment

- Students' questions should be relevant to the content.
- Confirm that students' answers are based upon the information presented in the text.
- If students infer answers to questions, confirm that they are based on information from the text and background knowledge relevant to the topic.

Adaptations

- If the lesson or chapter is lengthy, a specific number of pages may be assigned for completing the activity. Students can include the page numbers along with the text's title.
- When students complete the activity on their own, they should utilize books at their independent reading level. Since many text books are written 1-2 grade levels above the book's intended grade, struggling readers may need additional help interacting with the text. Textbooks intended for a lower grade level, covering the same unit of study, may be a resource.
- The activity may be used with a variety of informational text, e.g., magazines, websites, manuals, etc.
- Special education students or English language learners may complete the activity prior to classroom discussion, preferably with adult guidance. This allows them to build background knowledge and participate more fully in classroom discussion.
- Gifted students may select a question that was not answered in the text and research the question more thoroughly.
- Using this activity and high interest informational text with struggling readers allows the reader to be engaged in the reading process while teaching a reading comprehension strategy. Select text of personal interest, which capitalizes on students' background knowledge, and attend to the students' independent reading level.

Inferring Theme

Standards

✴ McREL Standards – Language Arts

(http://www.mcrel.org/standards-benchmarks/)

- Uses reading skills and strategies to understand and interpret a variety of literary texts
- Knows that themes recur across literary works

✴ Grade Levels: 3-5 (Ages 8-11)

Description

Comprehension is the ability to understand, remember and communicate ideas read. Active readers use comprehension strategies to make sense of text. Strategies include: inferring, making connections, determining importance, summarizing, questioning and synthesizing information. Active readers use many strategies as they read, one of them being inferring. When readers infer, they read between the lines using their background knowledge and clues from the text. Students will use this Kidspiration® activity to infer a text's theme.

Instructions

1. Explain to students that works of fiction and nonfiction contain themes. In most cases, a text will contain more than one theme. The *themes* are the big ideas and often carry emotion like sadness, joy or remorse. They are the *morals* or the *lessons* a text presents. Readers infer themes. Briefly retell the story of *Goldilocks and the Three Bears*. Ask students to infer the themes of this fairytale. Students' inferences will include: don't trespass, don't take things that aren't yours, don't be selfish, etc. Share that today they will use evidence from a text to infer the text's themes.

2. Go to **Kidspiration 3 Teacher menu>Teacher Resources Online>Lesson Plans** and open the *Inferring Themes.kia* activity, shown below, and review it with students.

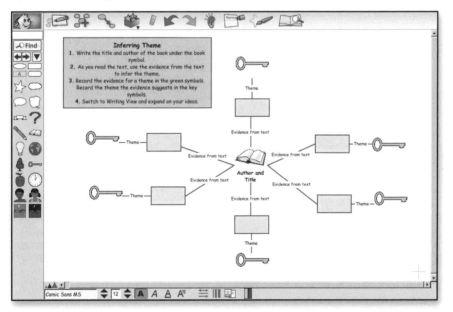

3. Select a text that contains several themes. Text suggestions are: Eve Bunting's *Going Home* or *Smokey Night* or *An Angel for Solomon Singer* by Cynthia Rylant.

4. Using a "think-aloud," model completing the activity. Stop at key points and share what evidence in the text is causing you to infer a specific theme. Record the evidence from the text in note form, followed by what theme the evidence suggests. Remind students again that the theme is the big idea, i.e., a moral or a lesson.

Note: If you would like to view an exemplar prior to teaching the lesson, view the *Inferring Theme Exemplar.kid* activity, shown below.

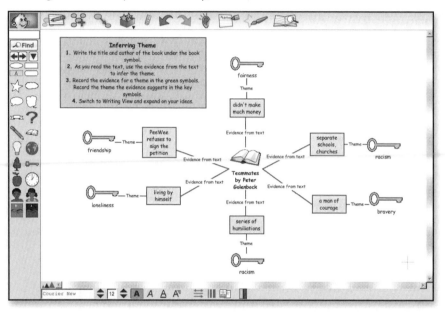

5. After reading the text, return to the activity and point out to students that the text contained many themes or big ideas, but for each theme the author's writing supported your thinking.

6. After students have had sufficient guided practice using the activity, have students complete the activity independently, reading text at their independent reading level.

7. After students have completed the activity, come back together and discuss the themes found in literature. Assist students in noting that themes reoccur in literature.

Additional comprehension lessons can be located here: **Kidspiration 3 Teacher menu>Teacher Resources Online>Lesson Plans.**

Assessment

- Students should have identified themes supported by the evidence in the text.

Adaptations

- When completing the activity independently, students should read books at their independent reading level.

- The activity may be used with nonfiction text as well.

Reading Reaction

Standards

★ McREL Standards – Language Arts

(http://www.mcrel.org/standards-benchmarks/)

- Uses reading skills and strategies to understand and interpret a variety of literary texts
- Knows that themes recur across literary works
- Makes connections between characters or simple events in a literary work and people or events in his or her own life

★ Grade Levels: 3-5 (Ages 8-11)

Description

Comprehension is the ability to understand, remember and communicate ideas read. Active readers use comprehension strategies to make sense of text. Strategies include: inferring, making connections, determining importance, summarizing, questioning and synthesizing information. Active readers are able to communicate thoughts about literary elements such as theme, and discuss their own insights after reading a text. Writing about what has been read moves readers to interact personally with the text and allows readers to synthesize. Synthesis integrates the readers own thoughts with the author's words and the reading achieves new insights. This Kidspiration® activity supports readers as they synthesize and discuss their insights about a text.

Instructions

1. Explain that active readers reflect upon what they read, continuing to think about the text after the reading is completed. Go to **Kidspiration 3 Teacher menu>Teacher Resources Online>Lesson Plans** and open the *Reading Reaction.kia* activity, shown below, and review it with students.

2. Share that active readers communicate their thoughts about literary elements such as theme, and often discuss their insights after reading a text through the use of writing. Writing about what has been read moves readers to interact personally with the text and allows readers to synthesize. Synthesis integrates the readers own thoughts with the words of the author and the reading achieves new insights. Further explain synthesis is a combination of the reader's background knowledge and the author's thoughts. After joining the two, new thoughts and insights are gained by the reader.

3. Using a "think-aloud," model completing the activity using a short text. Text that causes the readers to reflect or feel emotion are good selections to utilize. Suggested titles are: *Going Home* and *Fly Away Home* by Eve Bunting, or David Alder's *A Picture of Anne Frank*. When completing the *Personal Insight* portion of the writing, point out to students how you are using the author's words in addition to your own background knowledge to synthesize, developing new insights that the author didn't communicate in the text itself.

Note: If you would like to see an exemplar prior to teaching the lesson, open the *Reading Reaction Exemplar.kid* activity shown below.

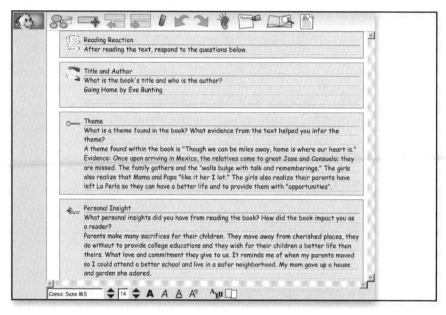

4. After students have had sufficient guided practice in completing the activity, they may complete the activity independently, reading text at their independent reading level. Remind students prior to use that active readers synthesize text. They take the ideas and words of the author, combine them with their own background knowledge, and gain new insights.

Additional comprehension lessons can be located here: **Kidspiration 3 Teacher menu>Teacher Resources Online>Lesson Plans.**

Assessment

- Students should have provided evidence of synthesis, including use of background knowledge and information from the text.

- Confirm that the theme identified is correct according to the text utilized.

- Questions should relate to the text and indicate use of higher cognitive processes.

Adaptations

- When completing the activity independently, students should read text at their independent reading level.

- The activity may be used with informational text as well.

- The literary element may be changed. For example, rather than asking students to comment on theme, they can identify and discuss use of figurative language.

Coding Text

Standards

✳ McREL Standards – Language Arts

(http://www.mcrel.org/standards-benchmarks/)

- Uses reading skills and strategies to understand and interpret a variety of literary texts

- Establishes a purpose for reading

✳ Grade Levels: 3-5 (Ages 8-11)

Description

Comprehension is the ability to understand, remember and communicate ideas read. Active readers use comprehension strategies to make sense of text. Strategies include: inferring, making connections, determining importance, summarizing, questioning and synthesizing information. Active readers use many strategies as they read. When students ask questions, whether it be before, during or after they read, it engages them in the reading process. Questions help readers clarify and understand what they read. Additionally, active readers are aware of their cognitive processes as they are reading. They "think about their thinking." In this Kidspiration® lesson, students ask questions and are cognitively aware of how their questions were answered.

Instructions

1. Explain that active readers use many strategies before, during, and after reading informational text, one of them being asking questions. Go to **Kidspiration 3 Teacher menu>Teacher Resources Online>Lesson Plans** and open the *Coding Text.kia* activity, shown below, and review it with students. Explain that readers are wondering many things as they are reading. Questions are generated from the illustrations and the text, as well as their background knowledge. Active readers are not only aware of the questions, but also aware of how their questions were answered. Because reading is thinking, readers need to become adept at being aware of their thinking. Today they will continue to learn to be aware of their thinking by asking questions and coding how their questions were answered.

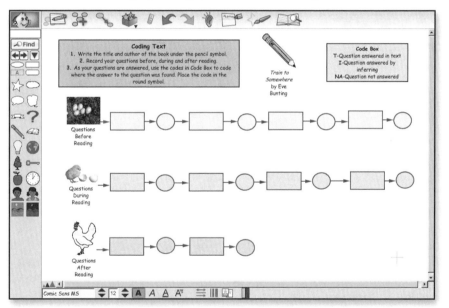

Note: Depending on previous comprehension lessons taught, you may decide to discuss the importance of readers asking "weighty" questions: questions that deepen the understanding of a text. For example, asking "I wonder why the girl has a blue dress?" does not deepen the meaning of the text for the reader. However asking "I wonder what caused the relationship between the two characters to change?" will deepen the meaning of the text as the reader reads to have the question answered.

2. Using a short text, model completing the activity. Text containing strong characters and a well-developed theme or plot work well. A suggested text is *Train to Somewhere* by Eve Bunting or *Charlie Anderson* by Barbara Abercrombie.

    Note: If you would like to view an exemplar prior to teaching the lesson, open the *Coding Text Exemplar.kid* activity shown below.

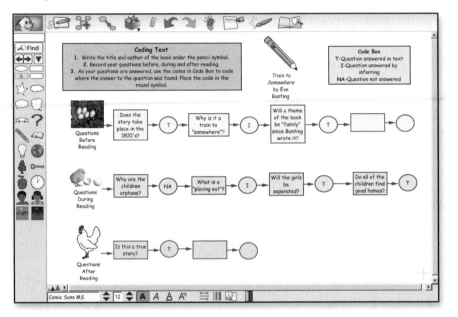

3. Record questions before, during and after reading in the corresponding symbols. Using the codes from the *Code Box*, record how the question was answered. Remind students that active readers are cognitively aware of how questions are answered. Active readers "think about their thinking" as they read.

4. Once students have had sufficient guided practice using the activity, have students complete the activity independently, reading text at their independent reading level.

Additional comprehension lessons can be located here: **Kidspiration 3 Teacher menu>Teacher Resources Online>Lesson Plans**.

Assessment

- Students should have followed the activity, asking questions relevant to the content.
- Confirm that students answers are coded based on the text read.

Adaptations

- More than one activity may be used for a text.
- Students may switch to **Writing View** to complete the activity.
- The activity may be used with a variety of informational text, e.g., magazines, websites, manuals, etc.
- Using this activity and high interest informational text with struggling readers allows the reader to be engaged in the reading process while teaching a reading comprehension strategy. Select text of personal interest, which capitalizes on students' background knowledge, and attend to the students' independent reading levels.

Literary Analysis

Standards

✴ McREL Standards – Language Arts

(http://www.mcrel.org/standards-benchmarks/)

- Uses reading skills and strategies to understand and interpret a variety of literary texts
- Understands elements of character development in literary works

✴ Grade Levels: 3-5 (Ages 8-11)

Description

Comprehension is the ability to understand, remember and communicate ideas read. Active readers use comprehension strategies to make sense of text. Strategies include: inferring, making connections, determining importance, summarizing, questioning and synthesizing information. Active readers read more deeply when they understand the use of literary elements. Literary analysis lessons are designed to help students become aware of and recognize the techniques and devices authors use to create works. This Kidspiration® activity will support the classroom curriculum related to literary analysis by providing a work space for students to record their analysis.

Instructions

1. Prior to beginning this lesson, decide which literary element will be explored. For the purpose of this lesson, character analysis will be used. This lesson may be replicated in additional lessons when other literary elements are taught. Go to **Kidspiration 3 Teacher menu>Teacher Resources Online>Lesson Plans** and open the *Literary Analysis.kia* activity, shown below, and review it with students.

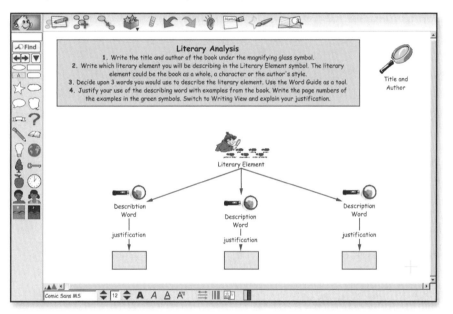

2. Share with students that when active readers analyze text, they explore how the author wrote the text, or the *author's craft*. When readers explore an author's craft, it can improve their own writing as well. Today they will explore how the author reveals a character to the reader by thinking about what the character says, does and thinks, and by what other characters say about him.

3. Select a text which reveals a character's traits through the aforementioned examples. A suggested text is *P.S. Longer Letter Later* by Danziger and Martin. The story is told entirely through letters, revealing the main character's traits. After reading the text, use a "think-aloud" to complete the activity. Ask students to describe the character, having them share their rational for describing the character as they did. Show students how to use the Kidspiration **Word Guide** to locate synonyms, selecting the best word choice to describe the character.

Note: If you would like to see an exemplar prior to teaching the lesson, open the *Literary Analysis Exemplar.kid* activity shown below.

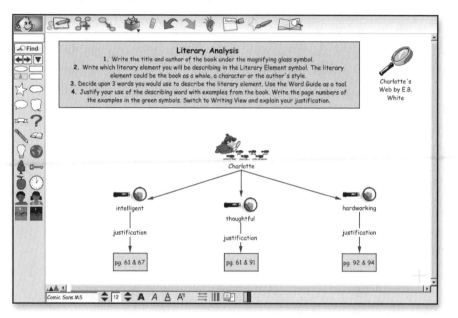

4. Once students have had sufficient guided practice using the activity, have students complete the activity independently, reading text at their independent reading level.

5. After students have completed the activity, come back together and discuss their analysis. Assist students in noting that characters can have many traits and many words can be used to describe the same trait.

Additional comprehension lessons can be located here: **Kidspiration 3 Teacher menu>Teacher Resources Online>Lesson Plans.**

Assessment

- Confirm that students have supported their analysis with evidence from the text.

Adaptations

- When completing the activity independently, students should read books at their independent reading level.

- The activity may be used with a variety of literary elements.

- The teacher may specify the number of examples from the text needed within the *justification* portions of the activity.

Determining Importance

Standards

✴ McREL Standards – Language Arts

(http://www.mcrel.org/standards-benchmarks/)

- Uses reading skills and strategies to understand and interpret a variety of literary texts
- Understands elements of character development in literary works
- Understands similarities and differences within and among literary works from various genre and cultures
- Understands the basic concept of plot

✴ Grade Levels: 3-5 (Ages 8-11)

Description

Comprehension is the ability to understand, remember and communicate ideas read. Active readers use comprehension strategies to make sense of text. Strategies include: inferring, making connections, determining importance, summarizing, questioning and synthesizing information. Active readers read more deeply when they understand the nuances of character and plot development. Readers understand and recognize that not all characters and events are of equal importance. This Kidspiration® activity will support readers as they reflect upon key story elements and evaluate their importance to the story.

Instructions

1. Prior to beginning this lesson, decide which key story element will be explored. For the purpose of this lesson, students will be asked to evaluate main and supporting characters. This lesson may be replicated in additional lessons when other key elements are taught and explored.

2. Go to **Kidspiration 3 Teacher menu>Teacher Resources Online>Lesson Plans** and open the *Determining Importance.kia* activity, shown below, and review it with students.

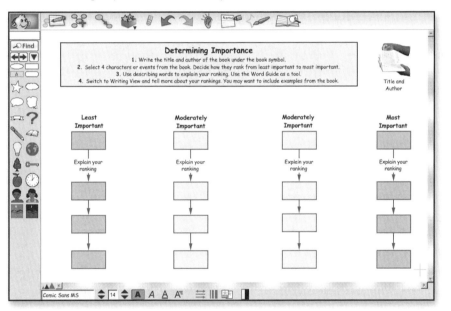

3. Share with students that active readers analyze text for the nuances and importance of characters or events. Today they will explore how the author reveals a character's importance within the story by analyzing the characters.

4. Select a short text which contains at least 4 characters. A suggested text is Eve Bunting's *Fly Away Home*. After reading the text, use a "think-aloud" to complete the activity. Ask students to rank the order of importance of the characters, having them share their rational.

Note: If you would like to see an exemplar prior to teaching the lesson, open the *Importance Exemplar.kid* activity shown below.

5. After students have had sufficient guided practice using the activity, have students complete the activity independently, reading text at their independent reading level.

6. After students have completed the activity, come back together and discuss their analysis. During the conversation, focus on why students ranked characters as they did.

Assessment

- Confirm that students have supported their rankings with evidence from the text.

Adaptations

- When completing the activity independently, students should read books at their independent reading level.

- The activity may be used with a variety of text, including biographies and autobiographies.

Confirming Predictions

Standards

✦ McREL Standards – Language Arts

(http://www.mcrel.org/standards-benchmarks/)

- Uses reading skills and strategies to understand and interpret a variety of literary texts

- Makes, confirms and revises simple predictions about what will be found in a text

✦ Grade Levels: 3-5 (Ages 8-11)

Description

Comprehension is the ability to understand, remember and communicate ideas read. Active readers use comprehension strategies to make sense of text. Strategies include: inferring, making connections, determining importance, summarizing, questioning and synthesizing information. Active readers use many strategies as they read. Making a prediction is similar to making an inference. Predictions are related to events or outcomes that are either confirmed or changed by the end of the story. Inferences remain unanswered and are left to the readers' interpretation. It is up to the teachers' discretion, taking into consideration the students' reading backgrounds and abilities, whether that information and level of detail is shared with the students during this lesson. Often the terms prediction and inference are used interchangeably depending on the age of the readers. Students will use this Kidspiration® activity to record their predictions and indicate whether their predictions were confirmed or changed by story's end.

Instructions

1. Go to **Kidspiration 3 Teacher menu>Teacher Resources Online>Lesson Plans** and open the *Confirming Predictions.kia* activity, shown below, and review it with students.

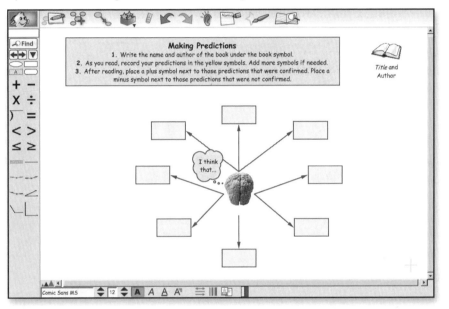

2. Explain that active readers make *predictions* and *inferences* while reading. Active readers *read between the lines* and use clues provided by the author. To demonstrate, pretend to order a pizza over the phone using words like: *medium, extra-cheese, thin crust* and *pepperoni*. Make sure to include an address while "placing your order" and ask, "How long will it be?" Do not use the word "pizza" in the role-playing. Ask students, "What have I just pretended to do?" They will answer, "Ordered pizza." Ask them how they knew given you never used the word "pizza." Students will respond by giving examples of the words you did use. Explain to them that they just "read between the lines." They made a prediction or an inference by using the clues you provided while role-playing ordering a pizza. Explain that active readers make predictions and inferences while they read, just as they did when you pretended to order a pizza. Further explain that they will look for clues and read between the lines in the following lesson. Remind students that authors provide clues in the text, as well as pictures.

3. Select a text which supports students making predictions and inferences. Text suggestions are: *Tight Times* by Barbara Shook Hazen, *Encounter* by Jane Yolen and Eve Bunting's *Fly Away Home*. Read the text aloud to students, stopping at key points and model making predictions.

Allow students to make predictions and inferences also. Record predictions on the activity.
Note: If you would like to view an exemplar prior to teaching the lesson, open the
Predictions Exemplar.kid activity shown below.

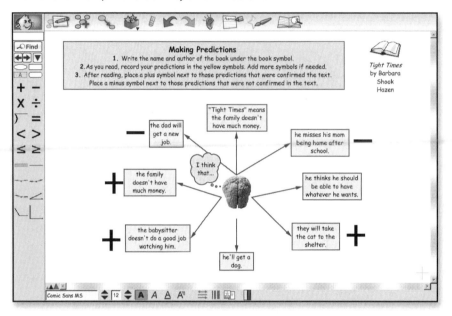

4. After reading the text, return to the activity and the predictions. From the *Math & Numbers >
   Math Symbols & Tools* library in the **Symbol palette**, drag an *addition* symbol
   next to the predictions that were confirmed during the reading of the text. In this case,
   you were able to confirm the prediction because the author stated it in the text. Drag a
   subtraction symbol next to predictions that were contradicted and changed during the
   reading of the text because the author stated otherwise. When modeling completing the
   activity, make sure to include predictions that were confirmed in the text and predictions
   that were contradicted or changed.

5. If you have explained the difference between a prediction and an inference, explain
   that statements without an addition or subtraction symbol are inferences. Inferences are
   predictions that weren't confirmed, contradicted or changed. If you have not explained the
   difference between a prediction and an inference, point out that readers don't always find
   out if their predictions were confirmed or need to be changed.

6. After students have had sufficient guided practice in completing the activity, have students
   complete the activity independently, reading text at their independent reading level.

Assessment

- Students should have made predictions and inferences that are appropriate to the text.

- Confirm that students' predictions and inferences can be explained and supported by text and/or pictures.

- Predictions should have either an addition or a subtraction sign next to them if appropriate.

Adaptations

- If utilizing a chapter book, an activity may be used for each chapter.

- When completing the activity independently, students should read books at their independent reading level.

- After completing the activity, have students who have a greater command of writing switch to **Writing View** and include the explanation for their predictions. Teachers may elect to have students color the addition and subtraction symbols, e.g., *green* for confirmed statements and *red* for unsupported statements. This allows the students to see which statements were confirmed or contradicted in **Writing View**.

- The activity may also be used with a variety of informational text, e.g., magazines, websites, manuals, etc.